Can Africans Do Economics?

Can Africans Do Economics?

Edited by Grieve Chelwa

inkani

This publication is published collaboratively by the International Union of Left Publishers (https://iulp.org/), and is issued under a Creative Commons Attribution-Share Alike 2.5 India (CC BY-SA 2.5 IN) license. The human-readable summary of the license is available at creativecommons.org/licenses/by-sa/2.5/in/

This edition published November 2024

ISBN 978-1-7764215-6-5

Edited by Efemia Chela
Proofread by Nkhensani Manabe
Cover designed by Kael Abello

Text set in Source Serif 4 by
Frank Grießhammer for Adobe

Inkani Books
2nd Floor, South Point Corner,
87 De Korte Street
Braamfontein,
Johannesburg,
South Africa,
2001

Inkani Books is the publishing division of
The Tricontinental Pan Africa NPC

inkanibooks.co.za

CONTENTS

ABBREVIATIONS

CCT Conditional Cash Transfers
CPI Consumer Price Index
DFID Department for International Development
EH Expectation Hypothesis
EU European Union
FDI Foreign Direct Investment
FISP Farmer Input Support Programme
FNDP Fifth National Development Plan
GDP Gross Domestic Product
ILO International Labour Organisation
IMF International Monetary Fund
IPL International Poverty Line
LFT Loanable Funds Theory
LPT Liquidity Preference Theory
MDG Millennium Development Goals
MMD Movement for Multiparty Democracy
MMT Modern Monetary Theory
NIEO New International Economic Order
NSPP National Social Protection Policy
OAU Organisation of African Unity
OECD Organisation for Economic Cooperation and Development
PRSPs Poverty Reduction Strategy Papers
PWAS Public Welfare Assistance Scheme
RBC Real Business Cycle
RCT Randomised Control Trials
SAPs Structural Adjustment Programmes
SDG Sustainable Development Goals
SMME Small, Medium and Micro Enterprises
SOEs State-owned Enterprises
TFP Total Factor Productivity
UCT Unconditional Cash Transfers
UN United Nations
UNCTAD United Nations Conference on Trade and Development
UNCEA United Nations Economic Commission for Africa
UNICEF United Nations International Children's Emergency Fund
WTO World Trade Organisation

Africa is Rich, not Poor

Vijay Prashad

Although most Africans are poor, our continent is potentially extremely rich. Our mineral resources, which are being exploited with foreign capital only to enrich foreign investors, range from gold and diamonds to uranium and petroleum. Our forests contain some of the finest woods to be grown anywhere. Our cash crops include cocoa, coffee, rubber, tobacco and cotton. As for power, which is an important factor in any economic development, Africa contains over 40% of the potential water power of the world, as compared with about 10% in Europe and 13% in North America. Yet so far, less than 1% has been developed. This is one of the reasons why we have in Africa the paradox of poverty in the midst of plenty, and scarcity in the midst of abundance.

Kwame Nkrumah, *I Speak of Freedom.*

Africa is a continent of at least 54 countries where over 3,000 languages are spoken. Nigeria, with a population of 220 million, accounts for over 500 languages alone. Although English is the official language of the country, a legacy of British colonialism, around ten per cent of the population speaks it as their first language (for half of Nigeria, Hausa and Yoruba, are their first language). The extraordinary diversity of the 1.4 billion people who live on the continent needs to be registered in the very first instance.

The experience of Kwame Nkrumah (1909–1972) as the leader of Ghana formed the basis for his insight in 1961 which, decades later, remains intact in our time. Africa is indeed a rich continent with a largely poor population. Estimates of Africa's natural resource wealth suggest that it is worth $6.5 trillion, at a minimum, but its total external debt is a fraction of that at $1.1 trillion. Because of debt, rooted in the neocolonial structure of the world system, half of the people on the African continent live in poverty. The existence of immense resources has not created wealth but instability and war, drummed up by colonialism and then the strong arm of multinational corporations (MNCs). An emblem of this paradox is that Africa contains 65% of the world's uncultivated arable land but is also reliant upon basic food imports. This enigma of concurrent wealth and poverty defines Africa's reality. Words such as corruption, inefficiency, and overregulation are frequently deployed to explain the situation, but they are only epiphenomenon.

Can Africans Do Economics? reflects on this fundamental problem of immense wealth and unpayable debt, of potential sovereignty and effective subordination. The title of the book is playful but real, echoing the actual confusion set in place by the assumptions made by mainstream economics and political science. Here are two of them: Africa's problems are endogenous, rooted in cultural factors and national liberation projects, and not exogenous, framed by the history of colonialism and the reality of the neocolonial world system. To claim that poverty is inherent in Africa is to exculpate colonialism and neocolonialism, which allow the continuation of this structure. There are of course several internal problems within African countries, as there are in any country, but these do not define the nature of the crises they face.

HOW AFRICA IS SEEN

In 2003, Thandika Mkandawire and Charles C. Soludo published an edited volume on the International Monetary Fund's Structural Adjustment Programmes (SAPs) imposed on Africa. *Imposed* is a strong word, but it adequately describes the zeitgeist of the 1980s and 1990s, and the essays by Marion Ouma and Cleopas Gabriel Sambo in this book make that very clear. In their introduction, Mkandawire and Soludo pointed out that the lack of belief Africans' capacity to build their own development agendas resulted in a deluge of over 100,000 foreign technical experts, costing over $4 billion annually to maintain have literally taken over the process of policy and project design and sometimes implementation. In what has ensued, Africa has turned into a pawn in the chessboard of experimentation for all manner of ill-digested development theories and pet hypotheses.[1]

The 'ill-digested development theories' emerge in two classic World Bank reports – *Sub-Saharan Africa: From Crisis to Sustainable Growth* (1989) and *Adjustment in Africa* (1994). By the late 1980s and into the early 1990s, the post-colonial national liberation frameworks that focused on undoing imperialism were set aside and multilateral agencies began to focus their attention on problems such as corruption, regulation, and a collapse of the rule of law. The overall framework of governance defined the problem narrowly and set aside the external problems of centuries of exploitation carried out by international powers.

The aftermath of the famine in Ethiopia (1983–1985) evoked an entire ensemble of stereotypes about Africa: poverty, hunger, corruption, disorder, and inefficiency. Out of disgust for this descriptive catalepsy Kenyan author Binyavanga Wainaina wrote his satirical 2005 essay, 'How to Write About Africa', which bitterly shows why the animals in *The Lion King* film have a more complex humanity than the humans in Karen Blixen's book *Out of Africa*.[2] It is commonly insinuated that if Africa's elites can be portrayed as rapacious, and its masses helpless, and if the continent can be reduced to the humiliations of poverty, then it makes sense that the West should re-colonise Africa through the multilateral institutions and their neoliberal reforms.

WHAT AFRICA MUST CONFRONT

Africa is weighed down by a buried history of colonialism, including the Atlantic Slave Trade, which stole wealth from the continent and used it to enrich Europe and the Americas. I express this history as *buried* because although it is widely acknowledged, this acknowledgement does not shape political responses to current crises. The wealth that could have been invested to solve basic problems was used instead to finance the industrial revolution in Europe and North America. This elementary point is not only an argument for better historiography but the importance of naming all impediments to development. African countries effectively must borrow money from the former colonial powers that stole African money. In turn, the money is borrowed at usurious interest rates and comes with onerous conditions which simply deepen debt rather than produce development.

Due to the insufficient decolonisation of the world economy, MNCs and former colonial powers use financial practices to enable the extraction of wealth from African states.[3] While the figures for this plunder have not been properly calculated, they would probably be in the hundreds of trillions from the 15th century to the 1960s alone. If one looks simply at illicit financial flows between 1980 and 2009, between $1.2 trillion to $1.4 trillion left the continent, equivalent to Africa's entire GDP of the continent, and far greater than the Foreign Direct Investment (FDI) that reaches its shores.[4]

African intellectuals and politicians confront two simultaneous problems. First, *structural pressures* of significant debt burdens and the swindle of FDI and development aid. SAPs forced countries to cut their subsidies for human development and their public wage bill, which meant a deterioration of public services (especially health and education) and the forced deregulation of the economy by the lack of state oversight. This, combined with the legal plunder authorised by MNC-controlled debates around accountancy and financial flows, opens the floodgates for the outflow of resource wealth.[5]

Second, *theoretical pressures* stem from an absolute denial of colonial theft and of the existence of an unjust world system. The scholars who have catalogued the deep impact of colonialism on Africa range from Walter Rodney, a Marxist who taught at the University of Dar es Salaam, Tanzania, to Kenneth Onwuka Dike, a liberal who was the first vice-chancellor of the University of Ibadan, Nigeria.[6] Despite their important work, the denial of colonialisation's impact shapes economic approaches to African countries. This denial means that the most important constraint for development is not permitted within the discourse on African economies and African development.

The theoretical pressure was deepened about five decades ago through two parallel developments. First, the almost deliberate disregard for the theories of national liberation that had emerged during the decolonisation movement. The work of these thinkers – from Nkrumah to Amílcar Cabral to Thomas Sankara – has been neglected, their books allowed to go out of print and their work not given the due regard for study. Without the lineage that runs from Nkrumah to Sankara, the theoretical armour needed to confront the imperialist logic of development simply cannot flourish.

That living tradition, which animates this book is directly elevated by several of the authors notably Ndongo Samba Sylla on Sankara and Grieve Chelwa on Nkrumah. The spirit of that tradition needs to be generated by a proper publishing programme (as has been conducted by Inkani Books) and must be returned to the centre of academic thought (there need to be more serious dissertations drawing from this lineage).[7] For this reason, Redge Nkosi's essay searches for a monetary policy fit for the reality of diverse African situations rather than importing a policy framework from colonising states. It is against that theoretical pressure that scholars such as Nkosi, and thousands of others in Africa, Asia, and Latin America, work to build policies against both the arrogance of IMF clichés, and the withdrawal into forms of nativism that cannot serve the needs of a modern economy.[8]

Second, the disregard of serious pan-African thought came alongside the attrition of the public universities on the African continent which had incubated Pan-Africanism. From the 1990s, public universities faced serious funding cuts, which forced them to rely upon finance from elsewhere for research. These entities included European, North American, and South African private foundations, funds from multilateral agencies (including those newly set up on the African continent, which received their own funding largely from European and US foundations), and money from EU coffers and USAID's largess. These funds were accompanied by their own constraints, which included fealty to the overall neoliberal research agenda.[9]

HOW TO SEE AFRICA

Can Africans Do Economics? emerges out of a process to recover the tradition of socialist Pan-African thought, rooted in the work of generations of scholars. Rather than provide a full assessment of that process, here are a few milestones achieved by those generations:

1. National liberation movements and their key intellectuals shaped an understanding of the continent as one marked by colonial structures and sensibilities, with plunder at its heart. These thinkers, from Kwame Nkrumah to Patrice Lumumba, from Julius Nyerere to Thomas Sankara, shaped an entire worldview that galvanised hundreds of millions of people into movements anchored by a socialist Pan-Africanist project. Ndongo Samba Sylla's chapter on Sankara explores the revolutionary ideas underpinning Burkina Faso's newly formed economy in the 1980s. A generation of scholars, even if they did not agree with the co-ordinates of Marxism, nonetheless worked in the shadow of the national liberation agenda.

2. Alongside the work of these movement intellectuals came intellectuals operating in many other spheres and public universities who accompanied the struggle but were not lodged in its institutional structures. Public universities opened departments, such as the Faculty of Arts and Social Sciences at the University of Dar es Salaam in 1964, to produce research relevant to the building needs of new African societies. Intellectuals involved in these sorts of endeavours created Pan-Africanist projects such as the Council for the Development of Social Science Research in Africa (Codesria) founded in 1973. Rooted in the science of their societies, these intellectuals produced a body of work that contradicted the Western development theory that saturated the IMF. (For instance, Henry Mopulo in Tanzania proved that the IMF-World Bank drive to increase productivity through capital intensive farming but without social transformation failed).[10]

3. Around the time of the 1985 United Nations 3rd World Conference on Women held in Nairobi, Kenya, a set of organisations and networks grew to emphasise the negative impact of SAPs on the lives of African women. These networks included Women in Nigeria formed in Lagos in 1982 by Bilkisu Yusuf, and African Women's Development and Communication Network (FEMNET) formed in Nairobi in 1988 by Njoki Wainaina. The voices of these women had

a decisive impact upon Sankara, who is acknowledged as one of the main national liberation leaders who took seriously women's political role and labour. Out of that tradition has emerged groups such as the Afrifem Macroeconomics Collective (NAWI), which intervenes in debates around macro-economic policy and whose core focus is the labour of working women.[11]

4. In the 1980s, a protest wave emerged across Africa against SAPs and policies that inflicted the full weight of austerity upon already poor people. The anti-IMF protests in Sudan in 1982 and then again in 1985, and demostrations in Nigeria through the summer of 1989 proved a point made in the Arusha Initiative of 1980. At the South-North Conference on the International Monetary System and the New International Order, a range of scholars and politicians from organisations such as the Third World Forum (Egypt), the Association of Third World Economists (Algeria and Cuba), and the Institute of Development Studies (Tanzania) published a call for a UN Conference on International Money and Finance. In the Arusha Initiative statement, they wrote:

> The IMF has proved to be a basically political institution. It tends to reproduce colonial relationships by constraining national efforts which promote basic structural transformations in favour of the majorities. Its orientation is fundamentally incompatible with an equitable conception of structural change, self-reliance and endogenous development. The IMF medicine systematically favours the more conservative sectors of society and traditional centres of power. Worse still, when these sectors constitute real national power alternatives, the fund prescriptions and its manner of dispensing them become an unabashed form of external political intervention in their favour. The fund's policies, conceived to achieve 'stabilisation', have in fact contributed to destabilisation and to the limitation of democratic processes.[12]

The UN conference that they proposed did not take place, and still has not taken place in the form that they required. Indeed, that is why a new generation of economists formed the Collective on

African Political Economy (CAPE) in April 2023, with a manifesto that echoes the Arusha Initiative in many of its formulations.[13] The power differentials in policy making are on stark display, with the IMF unfazed by criticism and willing to push for its 'medicine' regardless of the pain inflicted upon the masses. This book is, in many ways, a product of the frustration that led to the creation of CAPE.

5. Finally, out of the anger at how the Global North has blocked the advance of history has emerged several governments whose orientation is, strikingly, to advance the cause of their own people first. This includes several governments in the Sahel states (Burkina Faso, Mali, and Niger) that have formed the Alliance of Sahel States, and the government of Senegal. Each of these governments have made it clear that they want to put the interests of their people ahead of bondholders in the Global North. This desire for sovereignty is not restricted to the governments that could be called progressive. It is an emergent mood across the continent, as illustrated by the African Union's Peace and Security Council resolution in 2016 to forbid foreign military bases.[14]

But this mood, which derives from the national liberation era to the present, has not settled over monetary and industrial policy, which remain constrained by the structural and theoretical pressures of IMF thought. Thus far, three African Monetary and Economic Sovereignty Conferences have been held in Tunis (2019), Dakar (2022), and Addis Ababa (2024), out of which developed the African Heterodox Economics Network. These developments and the timely publication of this book signal a widespread desire for a new outlook towards economics on the continent.

ENDNOTES

1   *African Voices on Structural Adjustment. A Companion to Our Continent, Our Future*, eds. Thandika Mkandawire and Charles C. Soludo, (Dakar: Codesria) 2003.

2   Binyavanga Wainaina, 'How to Write About Africa', *Granta*, 92, 2005.

3   Ndongo Samba Sylla and Fanny Pigeaud, *Africa's Last Colonial Currency. The CFA Franc Story*, (London: Pluto) 2021.

4   African Development Bank and Global Financial Integrity, *Illicit Financial Flows and the Problem of Net Resource Transfers from Africa: 1980–2009*, Tunis: African Development Bank, 2013.

5   A series of studies by Tricontinental: Institute for Social Reseach have documented these structural constraints. These include *Life or Debt. The Stranglehold of Neocolonialism and Africa's Search for Alternatives*, Dossier no. 63 (April 2023) and *How Neoliberalism Wielded 'Corruption' to Privatise Life in Africa*, Dossier no. 82 (November 2024).

6   Walter Rodney, *A History of the Upper Guinea Coast 1545–1800*, Oxford: Clarendon Press, 1970 and K. O. Dike, *Trade and Politics in the Niger Delta, 1830–1885*, Oxford: Oxford University Press, 1956.

7   *The Revolutionary Thoughts of Kwame Nkrumah*, ed. Efemia Chela and Vijay Prashad, Johannesburg: Inkani Books, 2024; *Thomas Sankara Speaks. The Burkina Faso Revolution, 1983–1987*, (Johannesburg: Inkani Books) 2023; Amílcar Cabral, *Tell No Lies, Claim No Easy Victories*, (Johannesburg: Inkani Books) 2022.

8   For an attempt to thread the needle between these two extremes, see the special issue of *Africanus: Journal of Development Studies*, vol. 43, no. 2, 2013, in particular, the editorial by Sabelo J. Ndlovu-Gatsheni, 'Perhaps Decoloniality is the Answer? Critical Reflections on Development from a Decolonial Epistemic Perspective'.

9   Mahmood Mamdani, 'University Crisis and Reform: A Reflection on the African Experience', *Review of African Political Economy*, no. 58, 1993.

10 Henry Mapulo, 'The State and the Peasantry', *The State and the Working People in Tanzania*, ed. Issa Shivji, (Dakar: Codesria Books) 1985.

11 Gertrude Dzifa Torvikey, 'The Nawi Afrifem Collective; Bringing a Pan-African Feminist Voice to Macro-Level Economic Narratives in Africa', *Feminist Africa*, vol. 4, issue 2, 2023.

12 'The Arusha Initiative', *Development Dialogue*, vol. 2, 1980, p. 14.

13 For the CAPE manifesto, see Tricontinental: Institute for Social Research, *Life or Debt*.

14 Tricontinental: Institute for Social Research, *Defending Our Sovereignty: US Military Bases in Africa and the Future of African Unity*, Dossier no. 42, July 2021.

Development
as Emancipation

Grieve Chelwa

'Freedom and development are as completely linked together as are chicken and eggs! Without chickens you get no eggs; without eggs you soon have no chickens. Similarly, without freedom you get no development, and without development you very soon lose your freedom.'

Mwalimu Julius Nyerere, 'Uhuru na Maedeleo'
(Freedom and Development)[1]

At the close of the decade in 1969, a great many of countries in Africa had attained independence, ending the long period of subjugation and exploitation that was formalised by the Berlin Conference of 1884.[2] At that conference, the world's arch colonisers split up the continent among themselves with utter contempt for African people and their patterns of statehood that had existed up until that point. For this reason, the attainment of political independence, beginning with Egypt in 1922 and the inflection point that was Ghana in 1957, presented a palpable opportunity of starting anew and undoing the harm and humiliation of the past.

For many of the first generation of African independence leaders, political independence was viewed as the *sine qua non* of development. Osagyefo Kwame Nkrumah, the first president of Ghana and quite easily Africa's most iconic statesman, captured this notion well when he proclaimed 'seek ye first the political kingdom and all things shall be added onto it'.[3] Development was also seen as the essential ingredient that would consolidate the wider meaning and achievement of political independence. Mwalimu Julius Nyerere, the first president of Tanzania, had this to say in a speech aptly titled 'Uhuru na Maendeleo' ('Freedom and Development'):

> It is obvious [that freedom] depend[s] on social and economic development. To the extent that our country remains poor, and its people illiterate without understanding or strength, then our national freedom can be endangered by any foreign power which is better equipped. This is not only a question of military armaments – although if these are necessary, they have to be paid out of the wealth of the community. It is a question of consciousness among all the people of the nation that they are free men who have something to defend, whether the appropriate means of defence be by force of arms or by more subtle methods.[4]

In addition to articulating the symbiotic relationship between development and political independence, the first generation of leaders grasped that development was urgently needed. Nkrumah, for example, wrote in his autobiography:

> Once [political] freedom is gained, a greater task comes into view. All dependent territories are backward in education, in science, in agriculture, and in industry. The economic independence that should follow and maintain political independence demands every effort from the people, a total mobilization of brain and manpower resources. What other countries have taken three hundred years or more to achieve, a once dependent territory must try to accomplish in a generation if it is to survive.Unless it is, as it were, 'jet-propelled,' it will lag behind and then risk everything for which it has fought.[5]

For Mwalimu Nyerere, this fierce urgency of development required that African countries 'ran while others walked'.[6]

The distinguished Malawian economist Thandika Mkandawire understood that the thirst for development so well-articulated by Africa's independence leaders had motivations beyond merely increasing their people's material wellbeing. The quest for development was an emancipatory project aimed at overcoming the shackles of humiliation formalised by the Berlin Conference.[7] According to Mkandawire, many critiques, especially Western ones, of this developmentalist fervor on the African continent did not grasp that development and the 'catch up' aspirations driving it [were] not foreign impositions but part of Africa's responses to its own historical experiences and social needs [and have] much deeper historical roots and social support than is often recognized'.[8] To paraphrase Amartya Sen, development is freedom.[9]

What then is development? Mkandawire, for example, has argued that development means overcoming the indignities of colonialism.[10] For Sen, 'development can be seen ... as a process of expanding the real freedoms that people enjoy'.[11] Development, for example, means the freedom from being coerced into seeking one's meals in the rubbish pit. One sees here that Mkandawire and Sen's ideas of development imply one another. Development as dignity is *development as freedom*.

The landmark 1990 report from the South Commission, that was incidentally chaired by Nyerere, defined development as 'a process which enables human beings to realize their potential, build self-confidence, and lead lives of dignity and fulfillment. It is a process which frees people from the fear of want and exploitation. It is a movement away from political, economic, or social oppression. Through development, political independence acquires its true significance.'[12] Elsewhere the report expands on the notion of emancipation in this way: 'development is a process of self-reliant growth, achieved through the participation of the people acting in their own interests as they seem, and under their own control.'[13]

In his classic text *How Europe Underdeveloped Africa*, Walter Rodney makes explicit the link between development and emancipation. In discussing underdevelopment, Rodney writes:

> ...[a] more indispensable component of modern underdevelopment is that it expresses a particular relationship of exploitation: namely, the exploitation of one country by another. All of the countries named as 'underdeveloped' in the world are exploited by others; and the underdevelopment with which the world is now preoccupied is a product of ... exploitation.[14]

The quest for development is, therefore, a quest for emancipation. Development gives full meaning to self-determination, the clarion call for political independence in the run-up to the modal independence decade of the 1960s. This understanding of development as an emancipatory project is useful in assessing trends in development in Africa over the last three decades or so, a matter that we turn to in the next section. Further, it is critical for assessing the many 'development initiatives' that have been visited upon the African continent in the recent past.

IS AFRICA DEVELOPING?

The previous section has argued that development in the African case ought to be emancipatory. The question that then arises is what yardsticks shall we use to measure progress towards such a kind of development? The South Commission provided the following guidance: the 'first objective of [development] must be to end poverty, provide productive employment, and satisfy the basic needs of all the people, any surplus being fairly shared.'[15] Thus, even though development's goal is the achievement of the people's full personhood, dignity and autonomy, the practical definition provided by the Commission presents intermediate metrics that allow for the gauging of progress: Development must 'end poverty', 'provide employment', 'satisfy basic needs' and promote equality. These aspects can be viewed as important metrics for assessing whether a people are on the path towards the achievement of development.

On this score, is Africa developing?

To answer this question, we will rely on trends in poverty not because it is one of the most important metrics contained in the South Commission's report, but it is the one measure with an abundance of comparable data across space and time. In addition, as I argue later, meaningful reductions in poverty are synonymous with development as is understood here.[16]

In 1990, the World Bank introduced their a 'dollar a day' measure of poverty.[17] This measure was derived based on the cost of the lowest amount of calories required for sustenance, estimated at $1 per day or $370 per year. In this way, any person whose expenditure fell below 'a dollar a day' was considered poor. This so-called international poverty line (IPL) has subsequently been revised upwards in keeping with food price inflation and currently stands at $2.15 a day.[18]

There is much debate around the appropriateness of using the IPL to assess poverty. Philip Alston, who served as UN Special Rapporteur on extreme poverty and human rights from 2014 to 2020, issued a landmark report that was critical of the IPL.[19] According to Alston, the IPL was too low to correspond to any commonsense notions of what constituted poverty. And such an arbitrarily low poverty line has allowed many, such as the World Bank, to claim dramatic reductions in global poverty whose conclusions would be overturned were a higher and more reasonable poverty line used.

Criticisms notwithstanding, a big appeal of the IPL is that consistent data across the majority of countries has been collected since 1990. Even if it is reasonable and desirable to set higher poverty lines than the IPL, there currently isn't any such data that can support cross-country and cross-time analyses of poverty trends. Second, the incredible transformation of, for example, China's economy over the last 40 years has coincided with reductions in poverty measured using the IPL. China's poverty rate for 1981 was estimated at 88 per cent and by 2018 the poverty rate had reduced to 0.3 per cent, making this the fastest decline in poverty in history.[20]

There is a lot of evidence, not least from the Chinese government and Chinese scholars, showing that these reductions in poverty are real and not illusory in the sense that the lot of the typical Chinese person has meaningfully improved over the last four decades.[21] Many would agree with the conclusion that China's development transformation has been nothing short of emancipatory – the country now has a level of control over its destiny in ways that were unimaginable four decades ago. Whatever the limitations of the IPL, it has to be an indictment to have a great many of a polity's people living below such an absurdly low threshold. This makes poverty assessments important barometers in measuring progress towards development in the sense the word is used in this chapter.

In what follows, I present a series of charts that paint a picture of the story of poverty in Africa over the last three decades. The picture that emerges is not an encouraging one.

In 1990, two billion people across the world lived in poverty as defined by the IPL.[22] Three decades later, the number of the world's poor had reduced to 648 million people (see figure 1). This downward trend in the numbers of the poor was mirrored in all regions of the world except for Sub-Saharan Africa, whose trendline is visibly upward in Figure 1.[23] East Asia & the Pacific (EAP), a region that includes countries such as China, Malaysia, South Korea and Vietnam, witnessed some of the most dramatic reductions in the number of the poor. In 1990, close to a billion people in the EAP region lived in poverty and by 2019 that number had reduced to only 24 million people. South Asia, a region mostly dominated by India, also witnessed poverty reductions albeit at a slower pace than EAP. In South Asia, 600 million people lived in poverty in 1990. By 2019, the number of the poor had reduced to about 150 million people.

Number of People Living in Poverty (in Millions)

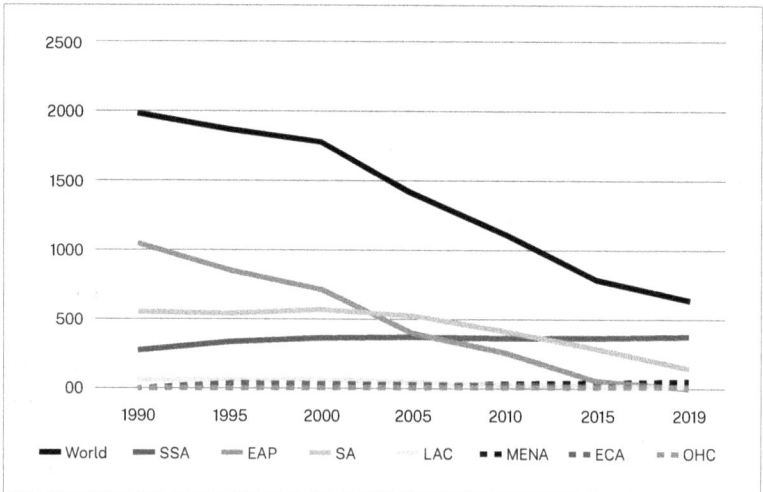

Figure 1

In Sub-Saharan Africa, the number of people living in poverty in 1990 was 270 million. After three decades, the ranks of the poor had grown by an additional 100 million bringing the population of the region's poor to 390 million in 2019. In 1990, only 15 per cent of the world's poor lived in Sub-Saharan Africa (see Figure 2). By 2019, Sub-Saharan Africa's contribution to the world's poor had grown by a factor of 4 to 60 per cent! Over the same period, East Asia and the Pacific's share declined from 50 per cent in 1990 to only 4 per cent in 2019. In other words, at the end of 2019, world poverty had largely become an African affair whereas in 1990 it was an East and South Asian problem.

Percent Share of World's Poor

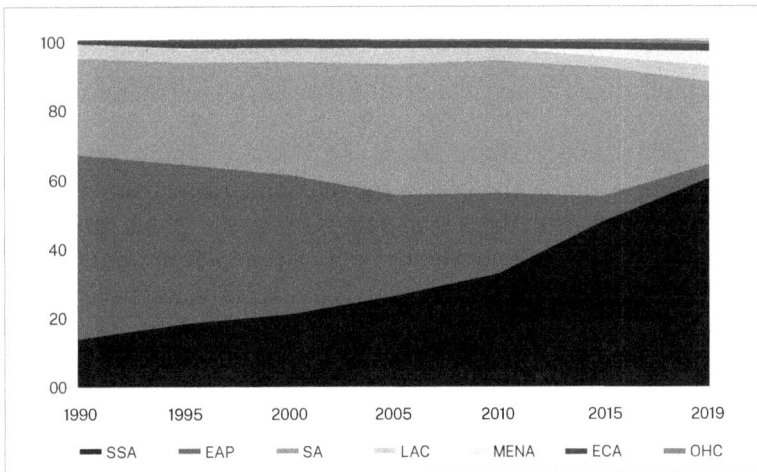

Figure 2

In terms of the poverty rate (the percent of a region's population in poverty) Sub-Saharan Africa has continued to lag other regions (see Figure 3). In 1990, our poverty rate of 53 per cent was only 1.3 times bigger than the world's poverty rate of 38 per cent. By 2019, Sub-Saharan Africa's poverty rate of 35 per cent, even though smaller than the 1990 number, was now 4 times bigger than the world's poverty rate of 8 per cent. Stated differently, the region's rate of decline in poverty was far slower than the decline in world poverty. This is also reflected in the trend lines in figure 3 that show that poverty rates in all regions of the world, with the exception of Sub-Saharan Africa, have declined and converged on single digits over the last three decades.

Poverty Rate

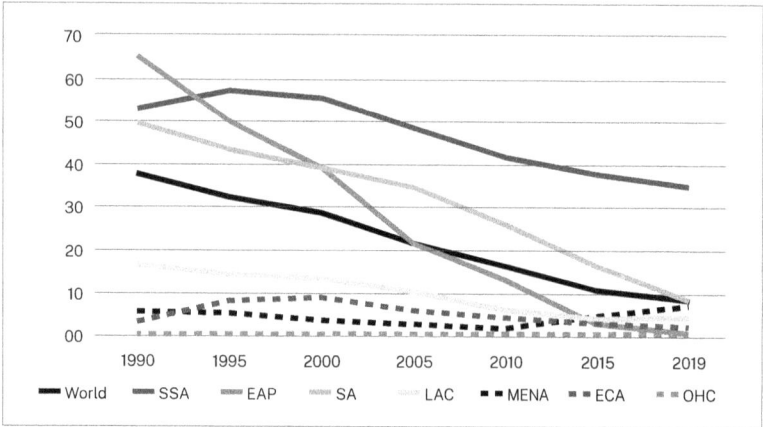

Figure 3

A final figure which showcases the dismal nature of the poverty story in Sub-Saharan Africa is contained in figure 4 which shows the percentage of the region's population living on $6.90 or less over the period 1990 to 2019. This higher poverty line is the typical poverty line in high-income countries where it is used as a criteria for the receipt of public assistance programmes. According to the figure, over the period 1990 to 2019, almost all of Sub-Saharan Africa's population would be considered poor and qualify for public assistance if they lived in a high-income country. In other words, the much-celebrated African middle class is a figment of our own imaginations going by high-income country standards.

Poverty Rate Using Higher Poverty Line

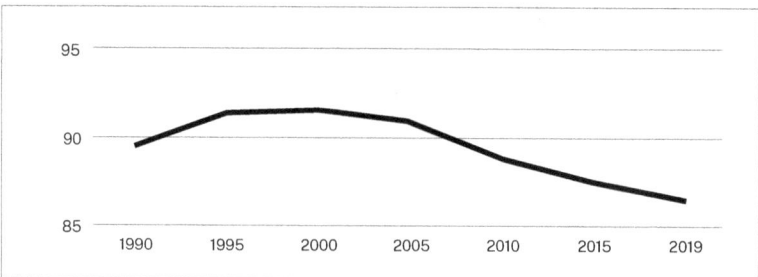

Figure 4

WHY IS AFRICA NOT DEVELOPING?

The previous section has documented some broad trends regarding the story of poverty and, by implication, development in Africa over the last three decades. Why is this unfortunate situation our story? How have some regions successfully reduced poverty or got solidly on the path to (if they have not already attained) emancipatory development whereas Africa has failed to do so? What accounts for this and what can be done about the situation?

As many scholars have so eloquently demonstrated Africa's underdevelopment as a structural process began with the continent's integration into the world capitalist system around about the 15th century. Ever since this integration, the continent's surplus value has been extracted and exported abroad to power and sustain economies elsewhere, especially in the western world. For close to 400 years until the abolishment of slavery and the slave trade in the 19th century, much of Africa's surplus was embodied in the form people trafficked against their will to the plantation economies of the so-called New World. In the New World, enslaved Africans were worked to the death growing the kind of crops, most notably cotton, that powered the Industrial Revolution.

After the abolition of slavery in the mid-19th Century, Euro-America's extraction of Africa's surplus relied on colonialism where the continent was carved up into colonies belonging to different European empires. Under colonialism, extracted surplus was embodied, not in the export of human beings as before, but in the export of raw materials directly from Africa that fed the industrialisation underway in Western Europe and North America.

Beginning in the early to mid-20th century, several factors combined that ultimately led to political independence in many African countries in the 1960s. First, many Africans participating and observing the Second World War came to view the Allied Forces' (mostly Britain and the US) rallying cry for the war, which was to free Europe from illegal German occupation, as hypocritical. During that era, most of the African continent, with very few exceptions, was under illegal occupation via colonialism. Second, the formation of the United Nations at the end of the Second World War was explicit in articulating a right to self-determination that came to inspire many independence movements in Africa. Third, the economics of the colonial model came to suggest that the economic returns from direct control were smaller than those that could be obtained under a system of indirect control. Owing to one or all these reasons, many countries in Africa were granted or fought for political independence that peaked in the 1960s.

With the advent of political independence, the extraction of the continent's surplus continued unabated and was facilitated indirectly via neocolonialism. Writing in 1965 in his magisterial text *Neocolonialism, The Last Stage of Imperialism*, Nkrumah described neocolonialism this way:

> The essence of neocolonialism is that the State which is subject to it is, in theory, independent and has all the outward trappings of international sovereignty. In reality its economic system and thus political policy is directed from outside. The methods and form of this direction can take many shapes ... The neo-colonialist State may be obliged to take the manufactured products of the imperialist power to the exclusion of competing products from elsewhere. Control over government policy in the neocolonial State may be secured by payments towards the cost of running the State, by the provision of civil servants in positions where they can dictate policy, and by monetary control over foreign exchange through the imposition of a banking system controlled by the imperial power. Where neocolonialism exists the power exercising control is often the State which formerly ruled the territory in question, but this is not necessarily so. For example, in the case of South Vietnam the former imperial power was France, but neocolonial control of the State has now gone to the United States. It is possible that neocolonial control may be exercised by a consortium of financial interests which are not specifically identifiable with any particular State. The control of the Congo by great international financial concerns is a case in point. The result of neo-colonialism is that foreign capital is used for the exploitation rather than the development of the less developed parts of the world. Investments under neo-colonialism increase rather than decrease the gap between the rich and the poor countries in the world.[24]

As theorised by Nkrumah, neocolonialism became the dominant form of extraction and impoverishment on the African continent following independence. Unlike colonialism where the presence of the coloniser was visible and palpable, neocolonialism is more subtle and harder to discern and, therefore it is difficult to rally the people against it.

As Nkrumah correctly observed, the typical feature of neocolonialism is the large inflow of foreign capital through so-called foreign direct investment (FDI) that exploits rather than develops. According to the United Nations Conference on Trade and Development (UNCTAD), the African continent received $580 billion in official development assistance between 1960 and 2005.[25] Over about the same period, the continent received FDI flows of some $150 billion.[26] However, this huge inflow of capital, which in total amounts to almost three-quarters of a trillion dollars, has coincided with the impoverishment of the continent as attested by the statistics in the previous section. Why has this large infusion of capital stymied the continent?

Two principal reasons, working through the channel of neocolonialism, explain why this phenomenon. First, the flow of official development assistance or aid has meant that a large army of aid workers and policy advisors from the West have come to dominate policymaking in Africa. Mkandawire has shown how this policy dominance harms efforts at development on the African continent. Writing in his important 1999 book *Our Continent, Our Future: African Perspectives on Structural Adjustment*, co-written with the Nigerian economist Charles Soludo, Mkandawire had this to say:

One reason for policy failure in Africa is simply that too many cooks have been in the policy-making kitchen ... No part of the developing world has had such a density and diversity of technical assistance as Africa. In some countries, ministries [are] literally partitioned among different donors. This [has] many implications. Not only [does] it tax the attention of the nascent African bureaucracies to the extreme, but it also [makes] the learning curve extremely costly. In the extreme cases, African policymakers [are] actually excluded from the learning process as donors [keep] the evaluations of the programs to themselves, either through exclusive distribution of the relevant documents or because of language barriers.[27]

Mkandawire and Soludo's observation were echoed by Adebayo Adedeji, the Nigerian economist who led the United Nations Economic Commission for Africa (UNECA) from 1975 to 1991. Adedeji, more direct about the sinister intentions of the 'aid industrial complex' than Mkandawire and Soludo declared:

> In many cases, our friends and development partners have been either unwilling or reluctant to grant us the elementary right to perceive for ourselves what is good for us and to assist us in realising our perceived goals and objectives. Often, they appear more interested in foisting on us their own perceptions and goals. When it comes to Africa, the outsiders have always behaved as if they know better than Africans what is good for Africa, and the result is that without the needed co-operation and support, Africa has particularly always been derailed from pursuing relentlessly and vigorously the agenda it has set for itself.[28]

In my own scholarship, I have documented how the problem of policy dominance is compounded by the fact that the influential research on the economics of the African continent, on which policy is based, is mostly conducted by western economists steeped in the tradition of neoliberal economics.[29] A striking feature of this research is the mental gymnastics that are performed in laying the blame at the foot of Africans without any mention of the very real machinations of neocolonialism.

A second channel through which neocolonialism impoverishes the continent is FDI. FDI, as distinguished from aid, constitutes private inflows of capital into Africa with the explicit intent of making an economic profit (i.e., extracting surplus). The primary reason why huge FDI flows into Africa have not had any discernable impact on the continent's development is that the target for FDI investments are the continent's valuable extractives or natural resources sector. According to UNCTAD, the majority of all the FDI flows into Africa between 1970 and 2005 went to the extractives sector.[30] Rather than aiding development, these types of investments have thwarted it in many ways.

First, the continent's many internecine conflicts are linked to the exploitation of natural resources. The classic example is the Democratic Republic of Congo where foreign-financed war has created violent and unstable conditions to easily spirit away the central African country's valuable minerals in addition to causing the deaths of millions of Congolese.

In other parts of the continent, foreign investors have been more subtle in causing the kinds of distractions needed to illicitly extract minerals. In countries like Nigeria, Ghana and Zambia, the approach has been to underwrite a local political elite that implements policies favourable to the foreign-owned extractives sector. Zambia, for example, has continuously granted its mining houses favourable tax treatments that rob the country hundreds of millions of dollars in potential tax revenue every year. In a puzzling policy move in 2021, the county ramped up its generous tax treatment of the mining houses while it was seeking a bailout from the International Monetary Fund (IMF). [31]

Further, foreign investors in the extractives sector prefer to invest only up to the point where they can export the commodities in their raw form with very little value-addition. This further robs the continent of considerable foreign exchange that could be earned from the exports of processed or semi-processed goods. Last, the fact that foreign investment into the extractives sector dwarfs investment in downstream activities (such as manufacturing) ties the continent's fortunes to the dangerous vagaries of the international commodity markets where prices swing, without warning, from one extreme to the other with devastating consequences for long-term planning.

THE FORGOTTEN STORY OF DEVELOPMENT IN AFRICA

A forgotten aspect of African economic performance is that many countries in the immediate post-independence period registered respectable economic performance that drove improvements in socio-economic development. Mkandawire and Soludo, who are one of the most careful documenters of this period, make the point that 'postcolonial African economic history is one of fairly respectable rates of growth for nearly a decade (including some 'miracles' in a number of countries)'.[32] They go on to write that 'between 1965 and 1974, annual growth in gross domestic product (GDP) per capita averaged 2.6% ... Changes in GDP per capita and changes in gross national product (GNP) ... clearly show an increase in per capita income up to 1980 ...'[33] These average statistics mask differences as in some cases African countries outperformed some of the best performing economies in the world. Writing elsewhere, Mkandawire makes this point in this way:

> It should be emphasized that the performance of the top performers in Africa was close to the best of the comparable Asian countries during that period. If one takes a growth rate of 6% over more than a decade as a measure of successful development performance, in the 1967–80 periods, ten countries enjoying such growth were African. These not only included mineral-rich countries such as Gabon, Botswana, Congo and Nigeria but also such countries as Kenya and Cote d'Ivoire, who slightly outperformed both Indonesia and Malaysia during the period.[34]

Mkandawire and Soludo note that with an increase in economic growth came an increase in 'investments in public schools, roads, hospitals and industries.'[35] Further, 'by the mid 1970s, many countries could point to significant progress in initiating processes of economic and social development. Some levels of industrialization had been initiated, levels of school enrolment had increased, new roads had been constructed, the indigenization of civil service had advanced...'[36]

The remarkable point to note in this brief period of post-independence economic success is that it largely came about by keeping neocolonialism at bay. First, much of the investment that came to power the impressive growth was mobilised from domestic savings.[37] This essentially meant that the post-independence state had to manoeuvre in deploying these investments beyond the extractives sector. Second, the fact that aid played a negligible role in capital formation meant the post-independence state entirely owned the policy process, therefore, was free to implement policies in line with its national objectives. Third, the impressive economic performance was on the back of import substitution industrialisation, showcasing the importance of industrialisation in the development process. Finally, this impressive economic performance was state-led – the direction of economic activity was not left to the market but steered by an activist state based on long-term planning.

The brief period of hopeful performance was cut short with the oil price shocks of the 1970s that sent many countries into balance of payments crises as they tried to cope with increasing import bills. Many countries unfortunately turned to the IMF for help, which was conditioned on countries committing economic suicide by implementing policies in direct opposition to the ones that had delivered dignifying economic growth and development in the immediate post-independence period. With the IMF and World Bank now fully in charge of the policy process, the stage was set for the astronomic increases in poverty that we have come to observe over the last three decades and documented earlier in figures 1 to 4.

THE FORGOTTEN PROMISE OF THE LAGOS PLAN OF ACTION

The effect of unfulfilled promises of global development strategies has been more sharply felt in Africa than in the other continents of the world. Indeed, rather than result in an improvement in the economic situation of the continent, successive strategies have made it stagnate and become more susceptible than other regions to the economic and social crises suffered by the industrialised countries. Thus, Africa is unable to point to any significant growth rate, or satisfactory index of general well-being, in the past 20 years. Faced with this situation, and determined to undertake measures for the basic restructuring of the economic base of our continent, we resolved to adopt a far-reaching regional approach based primarily on collective self-reliance.

Preamble of the Lagos Plan of Action[38]

In 1980, African heads of state and government gathered in Lagos, Nigeria for an extra-ordinary summit of the Organisation of African Unity (OAU). The summit had been called to take stock of the continent's economic development situation as it stood at the time. After two decades of political independence, economic self-determination had remained elusive with many countries just as dependent on their erstwhile colonisers as at the time of independence. Several international initiatives aimed at fostering transformative development had not yielded results. The much-heralded New International Economic Order (NIEO), adopted by the UN General Assembly in 1974, which was meant to provide a framework to end neocolonialism and economic dependency in the postcolonial countries, had failed to take off, prompting UN Secretary General Kurt Waldheim to issue the following words of disappointment in 1980:

> I do not need to recapitulate here the course that efforts to establish a new international economic order have taken over the last several years. On a number of occasions I have been driven to voice my disappointment ... the missing element is not technical knowledge or understanding. What has been lacking is the political will to make adjustments, evolve compromises and develop action-oriented strategies ...[39]

Against this background, the summit in Lagos gathered to discuss and adopt a new strategy meant to provide a blueprint for self-reliant development on the African continent in the coming decades. The strategy, which came to be fully known as the *Lagos Plan for Action for the Economic Development of Africa*, had been spearheaded by the UNECA under the leadership of the Nigerian economist Adebayo Adedeji. The plan's hallmark was to restructure the economic base of the continent in support of emancipatory development.

The Lagos Plan of Action addressed many matters of importance to the economic development of the continent. However, special pride of place was reserved for agriculture, industry, natural resources and banking and finance given how crucial these aspects were in building self-reliant emancipatory development.

Building a strong agricultural base was not only important for fostering self-sufficiency in food production but would be vital for providing the raw materials required by industry. Second, surpluses from agriculture would translate into the kind of savings that could drive the development of banking and finance and in turn finance the development of industry. In a similar way, the exploitation of natural resources (such as oil, copper, gold and cocoa) would generate surpluses that would directly finance the development of industry or indirectly, through fostering a strong banking and finance sector. Like agriculture, natural resources would also be important for providing raw materials for industry.

Crucially, the plan required that the development of banking and finance be driven by domestic savings to guarantee its insulation from foreign capital. As discussed earlier, foreign-owned banks were the handmaidens of foreign control and influence in Africa. In this way, the Plan presented an integrated sectoral and country approach to Africa's development.

It is worth noting that in the Lagos Plan of Action, the development of industry was the be-all and end-all of the plan. This was based on a correct reading of history that showed that successful attempts at emancipatory development were based on a strong industrial base. This is also the lesson of China whose unprecedented reduction in poverty and emergence as a self-determining global power has been driven by industrialisation.

Unfortunately, the Lagos Plan of Action was adopted right at the beginning of the economic crisis that came to define the African continent over the next four decades. The plan was eschewed in favor of structural adjustment plans drawn up by the IMF and World Bank whose intent and result was the removal of policy agency and sovereignty from Africa.

The fact that the Lagos Plan of Action was never implemented presents one of history's biggest missed opportunities for the continent.

CONCLUSION

The foregoing paints a picture of a continent that has struggled to attain emancipatory development. This, however, has not been for a lack of trying. Many of the first generation of African leaders articulated a coherent developmentalist ideology that saw total emancipation as the goal. Unfortunately, and unsurprisingly, the scourge of neocolonialism cut short this brief period of promise and today the African continent is more dependent on the rest of the world (especially the

West) than it was in the immediate aftermath of political independence. However, not all is lost. The various strategies for economic emancipation developed in the immediate post-independence period such as the Lagos Plan of Action and many national development plans contain the blueprint of what needs to be done if Africa is to attain emancipatory development in the 21st century.

ENDNOTES

1 *Julius Nyerere, Freedom and Development/Uhuru na Maendeleo: A Selection of Writings and Speeches, 1968-1973* (Dar es Salaam/London, Oxford University Press, 1973), 1–10.

2 Many studies consider Africa as referring primarily to the mass of land south of the Sahara Desert. In this chapter, I dispense with this strange practice and consider the continent in its entirety (North, South, West and East Africa).

3 As quoted in Kenneth W. Grundy, 'Nkrumah's Theory of Underdevelopment: An Analysis of Recurrent Themes', *World Politics* 15, no. 3 (July 2011): 439. It is worth pointing out that there is some debate about when the remarks may have been said. The quote refers to a statue, some say; in his biography others say the quote was heard on independence day.

4 Nyerere, *Freedom and Development/Uhuru na Maendeleo*, 1.

5 As quoted in Grundy, 'Nkrumah's Theory of Underdevelopment', 457.

6 Thandika Mkandawire, 'Running while others walk: Knowledge and the Challenge of Africa's Development, *Africa Development* 36, no. 2 (2011): 1–36.

7 Mkandawire, 'Running while others walk'.

8 Mkandawire, 'Running while others walk'.

9 Amartya Sen, *Development as Freedom* (New York: Anchor Books, 2000).

10 Mkandawire, 'Running while others walk'.

11 Sen, *Development as Freedom*, 3.

12 South Commission, *The Challenge to the South: The Report of the South Commission* (Oxford: Oxford University Press, 1990), 10.

13 South Commission, *Challenge to the South*, 13.

14 Walter Rodney, *How Europe Underdeveloped Africa* (London: Bogle-L'Ouverture, 1972), 14.

15 South Commission, *The Challenge to the South*, 13.

16 Additionally, the widely lauded Sustainable Development Goals of the United Nations has 'ending poverty in all its forms everywhere' as goal number one. See 'Ending poverty in all its forms everywhere,' The United Nations, accessed March 11, 2024, https://sdgs.un.org/goals/goal1.

17 World Bank, *World Development Report* (Washington, DC, World Bank, 1990).

18 World Bank, *Poverty and Shared Prosperity* (Washington, DC, World Bank, 2022).

19 Philip Alston, *The Parlous State of Poverty Eradication: A Report of the Special Rapporteur on Extreme Poverty and Human Rights* (New York, United Nations, 2020).

20   World Bank and the Development Research Center of the State Council of the People's Republic of China, *Four Decades of Poverty Reduction in China: Drivers, Insights for the World, and the Way Ahead* (Washington, DC/Beijing, World Bank, 2022).

21   See World Bank and Development Research Center, Four Decades of Poverty Reduction in China; Zhang Weiwei, *The China Wave: Rise of a Civilization State* (Hackensack, NJ, World Century Publishing Corporation, 2011).

22   'Poverty and Inequality Platform', World Bank, accessed March 11, 2024, https://pip.worldbank.org/home.

23   The World Bank, and many other international agencies, like to separate the continent into Sub Saharan Africa and North Africa. The latter is then grouped with the Middle East.

24   Kwame Nkrumah, *Neo-Colonialism, The Last Stage of Imperialism* (London, Thomas Nelson and Sons, 1965), ix–x .

25   United Nations Conference on Trade and Development (UNCTAD), *Economic Development in Africa: Doubling Aid: Making the Big Push work* (Geneva/New York, United Nations, 2006).

26   United Nations Conference on Trade and Development (UNCTAD), *Economic Development in Africa: Rethinking the Role of Foreign Direct Investment* (Geneva/New York, United Nations, 2005).

27   Thandika Mkandawire and Charles C. Soludo, *Our Continent, Our Future: African Perspectives on Structural Adjustment* (Trenton, NJ/Dakar, Africa World Press and CODESRIA, 1999), 35–36.

28   Mkandawire and Soludo, *Our Continent, Our Future*, 36.

29   See Grieve Chelwa, 'Does Economics have an "Africa Problem"?' *Economy and Society* 50, no. 1 (February 2021): 78–99.

30   UNCTAD, *Economic Development in Africa*.

31   'IMF Deal: Cry My Beloved Zambia,' Grieve Chelwa, accessed March 11, 2024, https://gchelwa.substack.com/p/imf-deal-cry-my-beloved-zambiahtml.

32   Mkandawire and Soludo, *Our Continent, Our Future*, 5.

33   Mkandawire and Soludo, *Our Continent, Our Future*, 6.

34   Thandika Mkandawire, 'Thinking about Developmental States in Africa,' *Cambridge Journal of Economics* 25, no. 3 (May 2001): 303.

35   Mkandawire and Soludo, *Our Continent, Our Future*, 36.

36   Mkandawire, 'Thinking about Developmental States in Africa'.

37   Mkandawire, 'Thinking about Developmental States in Africa'.

38   Organisation of African Unity, *Lagos Plan of Action for the Economic Development of Africa: 1980 to 2000* (Addis Ababa, OAU, 1980), 4.

39   Quoted in Rose M. D'Sa, 'The Lagos Plan of Action – Legal Mechanisms for Co-operation between the Organisation of African Unity and the United Nations Economic Commission for Africa,' *Journal of African Law* 27, no. 1 (Spring, 1983): 13.

Re-defining Social Policy in Africa in the Era of Cash Transfers

Marion Ouma

Over the last two decades, social protection policies have risen in popularity in the social development agenda and most development agendas are judged to be incomplete without them. While the idea of cash transfers features most prominently as a component of social protection, social protection itself is a subset of social policy. Social policy is defined as 'collective public efforts aimed at affecting and protecting the social wellbeing of people in a given territory.'[1] In practice, it refers to mechanisms through which states ensure the provision of goods and services to improve the wellbeing of their people.

Social policy therefore encompasses aspects related to the provision of healthcare, education, housing and social protection among others. The role of social policy largely rests on governments, who through revenue collection, deploy resources to meet the needs of their citizens. The responsibility to meet these obligations may also be performed by non-state actors including non-governmental organisations (NGOs), faith-based entities and individuals. Social policy is important as, along with attendant programmes, it forms the cornerstone of interventions to reduce poverty and vulnerability, enhance redistribution, and promote state building.[2][3][4]

Despite the varying definitions of social protection, most standard interpretations tend to mention poverty reduction, vulnerability and enhancing resilience as core aims. The International Labour Organisation (ILO) defines social protection using the notion of 'floors.' They write,

... social protection floors, containing basic social security guarantees that ensure that over the life cycle, all in need can afford and have access to essential health care and have income security at least at a nationally defined minimum level. Social protection floor policies should aim at facilitating effective access to essential goods and services, promote productive economic activity and be implemented in close coordination with other policies enhancing employability, reducing informality and precariousness, creating decent jobs and promoting entrepreneurship.[5]

This definition mirrors the role of ILO in supporting labour relations based on its tripartite relationship with workers and employers. Meanwhile, the World Bank's definition is centred on the notion of safety nets as public measures to protect against the effects of economic and social distress on households and individuals.

With the rise of cash transfers within global development and their popularisation by international organisations, cash provisions now form a large part of development and humanitarian interventions eclipsing other social protection components such as social insurance or even health insurance. Other social protection programmes include labour regulations and in-kind transfers like school feeding programmes, provision of fertiliser and seeds, and subsidies. The hype around cash transfers has narrowed social policy to social protection, with a further narrowing of social protection to cash transfers.

Cash transfers can be provided either as conditional cash transfers (CCT) or as unconditional cash transfers (UCT). With CCT, beneficiaries are often required to meet certain conditions before receiving further payments. Requirements are often tied to human development targets which may include regular school attendance or immunisation visits at antenatal clinics. Adherents of CCT programmes argue that the requirements support families to acquire better health, education and other capabilities.

In contrast, UCT programmes make no conditional obligations on beneficiaries; payments are made with no demands. Interestingly, research conducted indicates that even without conditionalities, households still do take their children to school and for health services.[6] CCT has largely been used in Latin America whereas in

Africa, governments and international organisations have not tied the provision of cash transfers to conditionalities.

Cash transfer programmes are often not universally accessible but targeted to specific groups of people. In most cases, cash transfers are paid to children, older persons or people with disabilities. Even within these groups, cash is not provided to whole populations but is instead directed at a small number of people within the category. For instance, cash transfers for elderly people may be provided only for people over 70 years old who are not entitled to any other support such as pensions.

Targeting is often based on proxy means measures which rank populations, with the poorest of the poor qualifying for these programmes. In some cases, cash may be provided to pregnant and breastfeeding mothers, girls, farmers, or sex workers as part of experiments such as randomised control trials (RCT). Debates about the efficacy and effects of different targeting mechanisms exist in tension with other debates around the need to provide universal rather than targeted provisions.[7][8][9] On one hand, due to limited financial resources, programmes can only reach a limited number of people so targeting is necessary. On the other hand, persistent levels of poverty require universal provisions and universal programmes enhance equitable access to services. I will explore both ideas later in this essay.

Cash transfers, promoted as the new frontier in social development and the 'silver bullet' for poverty, have been adopted by African governments as tools to improve society and meet humanitarian needs. Providing cash transfers, it is promised, will also reduce rates of child mortality, teenage pregnancy, the prevalence of HIV/AIDS, and improve education. In terms of the Millennium Development Goals (MDGs), cash transfers were explicitly linked to MDG 1 concerned with halving poverty.

However, this ambition was not realised by the end of the MDG programme in 2015. (The MDGs have been superseded by the Sustainable Development Goals). Estimates indicate that for African countries there was an increase in the number of people living in poverty up from 420 million in 2018 to 424 million in 2019.[10] International organisations, particularly the UN, have been at the forefront of urging governments to adopt cash transfers to enable the attainment of SDGs as well.

In humanitarian situations, aid workers are increasingly using cash transfers to provide for communities experiencing catastrophes such as famine, earthquakes and floods. For instance, following the February 2023 earthquake in Türkiye, UNICEF estimated that it would 'reach 500 000 households with cash transfers' to provide relief for victims of the devastation.[11] Departing from traditional modes of humanitarian assistance that included food supplies, water and tents, international agencies now more often provide cash to those affected in lieu of material goods. Survivors of disasters are then expected to use the cash to purchase food and other essential items. Aid workers argue that unlike traditional forms of social provisioning, cash provides recipients with the choice and freedom to acquire what they need. During the global COVID-19 pandemic, most governments adopted and expanded the use of cash transfers to deal with the economic and social impacts, further propelling the narrative of the superiority of cash transfers programmes.

AFRICA AND THE NEOLIBERAL TURN

Today, most African nations have some sort of cash transfer programme in place, perhaps the culmination of a trend that started two decades ago. In some countries, multiple cash transfers are rolled out at the same time. In Kenya, for example, under the National Safety Net Programme the government is implementing the Cash Transfer for Orphans and Vulnerable Children, the Hunger Safety Net Programme and the Older Persons Cash Transfer Programme.[12] In-country these programmes are implemented by governments in partnership with international NGOs. The influence of international organisations on African social policy, however, has a longer history.

In the late 1970s and 1980s, African countries underwent economic and social reforms popularly referred to as structural adjustment programmes (SAPs). The reforms followed a period of sustained growth and improvement in the living standards of Africans after independence.[13][14] With independence, governments across the continent made intentional effort to improve the welfare of their citizens. To achieve this, investment was made in education, health and agriculture resulting in a rise in education attainment, a reduction in child mortality rates and general improvement in nutrition. Sociologist Jimi Adésínà demonstrates how investment in social expenditure by governments in Tanzania, Ghana and Nigeria improved health outcomes in the three countries.[15]

Coming from the colonial period when basic social services were provided based on race or through employment, post-colonial governments expanded access to the basic services for previously neglected Africans. This was driven by a need to create a well-educated, healthy population capable of taking over the colonial state. Of chief importance though, was the desire to improve people's wellbeing and dignity. The universal approach to social service provision embraced by the governments at the time, aimed to achieve developmental goals but was also undertaken as part of the nation-building agenda.[16]

This period of state-led social policy interventions was short-lived as states were forced to cut social spending as part of structural adjustment prescriptions. According to the Bretton Woods institutions, adjustment interventions were necessitated by the wanton spending of African governments. However, this analysis of Africa's financial and debt crisis and the policy solutions offered were faulty. As economist Jason Hickel notes, the financial crises governments found themselves in were brought about by an unequal balance of trade that endures to the present day.[17]

The integration of African economies in global trade after independence perpetuated the extraction of African resources by merely shifting how it was conducted within a sanctioned process of globalisation. Exploitative terms of trade meant that African countries continued to be primary suppliers of raw materials in the global market while importing manufactured goods from the Global North. Within the controlled trade regime, the drop in primary commodity prices dealt a further blow to primary goods suppliers. Unable to meet both national and international debt obligations, governments had to resort to the IMF and the World Bank.

Premised on the idea of 'cutting your coat according to your size' the two organisations instituted SAPs where they would provide loans to governments on the basis that they undertook stabilisation, liberalisation, and privatisation of their economies. The policy prescriptions were the removal of state subsidies, cost sharing arrangements for public goods and services, selling of parastatals, retrenchment and freezes on increase of wages and government employment. Many scholars have noted that financial crises did not only affect countries in the Global South; those in the Global North were affected as well, though to a lesser extent.[18] However, SAPs were only imposed in the Global South depicting the double standards that structure the world economy.

The result of structural adjustment was that 'economies shrank, incomes collapsed, millions of people were dispossessed, and poverty rates shot through the roof. Global South countries lost an average of $480 billion per year in potential GDP during adjustment period.'[19] Due to cuts made to social spending budgets, individuals were expected to pay fees for education, medical supplies and other services previously provided by the state. Job retrenchment, privatised government parastatals and the freeze on state employment meant that many households lost their primary sources of income and could not meet their basic needs. To cope with the rising cost of living, people resorted to self-employment leading to high rates of precarious or informal labour.

The crisis deepened as it coincided with the HIV/AIDS epidemic which ravaged the continent in the 1980s and 1990s. The deepening health crisis, increased poverty levels and vulnerability resulted in a polycrisis which governments and communities found hard to manage. Meanwhile, the role of state changed from a 'providing state' to a 'night watchman state' as its role shrunk to creating a conducive environment for markets to operate.

The foundation of the current wave of social protection programmes in the form of cash transfers is a response to the effects of SAPs. With countries having to cut down social spending, poverty rates increased leading to unrest and riots in countries such as Zambia in 1986, Nigeria in 1989, Niger in 1991, and Kenya in 1990.[20] This included riots by workers but also by university students protesting hikes in fees. As far back as 1987, a UNICEF report called *Adjustment with Human Face*, exposed the suffering brought about by SAPs on families and children.[21] African scholars had already been challenging the suitability of SAPs in their countries, and along with activists they called for a cessation and reform of the stabilisation process.

Following the 'success' of cash transfers in Latin America to alleviate poverty reduction and issues such as destitution, the Bretton Woods institutions transferred the strategy to Africa in the 2000s to deal with disastrous effects of SAPs and quell the rising unrest caused by the increased cost of living. In the interim, between the independence wave of the 1960s–1970s and the 2000s, many African countries had become fully authoritarian or had leaders who stifled democracy or enforced political repression. The rising social unrest soon morphed into political agitation with the clamour for multi-party democracy at its core in places such as Zambia and Kenya. With political instability imminent, the response of the international multilateral organisations was the provision of targeted social assistance to the poorest and the concept of safety nets and cash transfers grounded in the World Bank's Social Risk Management framework.

Cash transfers became a popular mode of support first in Latin America where the governments of Brazil and Mexico introduced the *Bolsa Família* (Family Allowance) and *Oportunidades* (or Prospera) social assistance programmes respectively.[22][23] This kind of social protection intervention made its way to the continent, but it was not entirely new as South Africa and Namibia, for instance, had some forms of transfers on-going since 1928 and 1998 respectively.[24] Starting in the early 2000s, this wave of cash transfers was introduced in Zambia with the help of GIZ (the German International Co-operation Agency) and Kenya via UNICEF. The projects at the time comprised of small pilot programmes and with time, international organisations expanded to the entirety of the African continent.

THE ORIGINS OF THE CASH TRANSFER IDEOLOGY

Several sentiments about cash transfers have worked to create hype around them. Current proponents of cash transfers couch it as a 'new revolution', 'a silent revolution', and a form of ingenuity in the era of poverty reduction. But cash transfers as an idea stretch far back into the history of neoliberalism. The idea of providing cash transfers can be traced to a group of scholars known as the Mont Pelerin Society formed in 1947 which comprised of economists such as Fredrich von Hayek, Milton Friedman and others who believed in *laissez-faire* capitalism.[25] von Hayek believed that a pure market was an efficient mechanism for the distribution of wealth and goods.

It could operate without human distortions and be a place 'where everyone acting in their own self-interest would yield maximum benefits for all.'[26] This ideology of the free market came to be known as neoliberalism and it is viewed as superior for the market to be in charge of service provision instead of the government taking on that role or interfering in the market.

In his highly influential book, *The Road to Serfdom*, Hayek emphasised that government provision enslaves people to services they do not need and also provides services in unsuitable ways.[27] He argued that instead people should be left to decide how they want to live their lives by making their choices through markets. Hayek's ideas resonated with those of his friend Milton Friedman. Friedman became the champion for the limited state, making the view more popular among the political class. He was instrumental in transferring the idea of a limited state from its Austrian roots to the US. Following World War I, the American government introduced the New Deal, a vast programme of government-funded projects which included public works with good wages to stimulate demand. After WWII, with Keynesian principles starting to fray, Friedman found space to promote Hayekian ideas. He, along with other think tanks and research institutions, such as the Institute for Economic Affairs, agitated for the abandonment of the New Deal and encouraged the state to cut spending on social services.

The ascendancy of Prime Minister Margaret Thatcher in 1979 in the UK and the election of US President Ronald Reagan in 1981 cemented the neoliberal ideas promoted by Hayek and Friedman.[28] [29] Both leaders are credited with fortifying neoliberalism within political discourse and practice. During their tenure, they ensured cuts in social spending and an erosion of trade union power. Their support for neoliberalism also spread beyond their borders, to the rest of the world manifesting in SAPs.

What started as an intellectual concept became the cornerstone of IMF and World Bank prescriptions to countries in the Global South. Markets became the primary provider of education, health services and agriculture extension services. For the poorest, cash transfers became the means to access market-based goods and services. Central to Hayek's propositions is also the notion of freedom, the same view held by cash transfer advocates who argue that they provide freedom to beneficiaries. Proponents also argue that individuals are best placed to choose what is suitable for their needs as they are better stewards of their lives. The argument runs counter to other views that the state should provide basic services. In fact, this view argues that government provision curtails freedom and choice and undermines personal dignity.

THE IMPACT OF INTERNATIONAL ORGANISATION-LED SOCIAL POLICY

Recent research on cash transfers has focused on the political economy of the programmes how they were adopted by states. Fleshing out the current views on these processes expands our understanding of geopolitical influences on social policy in Africa. Three strands of research attempt to explain the trend towards cash transfers. First, some scholars argue that social protection and cash transfer programmes were the result of national political processes within African countries. Researchers working on this body of knowledge use the political settlements framework and assert that the adoption of cash transfers is driven by African political elites to keep power or to get into power.[30][31] However, the claims that African governments adopted cash transfers to gain patronage and stay in power are an over-exaggeration.

In most countries, cash transfers do not reach a significant enough number of voters who would be able to influence the outcome of an election. Social protection and cash transfers have only recently started featuring in political and election manifestos but are still not salient enough in campaign agendas. Moreover, for a number of countries, cash transfer schemes are still fully donor funded. Even though governments have increased financial budgets for cash transfers, the programmes remain largely the domain of international organisations. It is difficult to argue that they are a symptom of patronage politics.

Another strand of research argues that the rise of cash transfer schemes was a result of policy learning where international organisations transferred the policy through learning activities that included study tours, workshops and seminars. This narrative portrays learning as a benign process but, in reality, learning regularly happens in uneven power dynamics where the bearer of knowledge has some power over the learner. Learning is therefore a site of power as Adesina explains:

> Learning is more than a benign exchange among intellectual and policymakers or medium for policy learning. Ideas may serve the function of seizing control of the policy terrain, undermining policy learning; generating policy atrophy in the host local context, distorting local realities, and undermining long-term sustainable development.[32]

Policy learning alone cannot sufficiently explain the uptake of cash transfers on the continent without consideration of how power operates in policymaking spaces as well.

The third research strand focuses on the role of international organisations as powerful policy proposers. Scholars argue that organisations like the World Bank, UNICEF and DFID used powerful mechanisms to drive the implementation of cash transfers.[33] Using their considerable knowledge, financial resources and their superior position in the global structure, they have manipulated countries to carry out certain policies.

Some mechanisms they have employed include promising wider budget support and financial incentives if cash transfers schemes were expanded, policy learning and controlling the interests of policymakers. Governments resisting the trend are often labelled as lacking political will. Overall, the enduring legacy of unequal power relations between countries in the global south and international organisations harms our development as a continent.

THE LIMITATIONS OF CASH TRANSFERS

Despite their benefits, questions abound over whether cash transfers are the most appropriate mode of social policy provision. The promotion of cash transfers, it can be said, has led to the diminution of social policy instead of enabling a broader conception of social protection. One of the limitations of cash transfers discourse is the over-reliance on a single instrument which has crowded out the thinking around other forms of social policies that have more redistributive effects. To propel the adoption of cash transfers in African countries, international organisations have ignored studies that indicate that the implementation of labour laws, particularly those that enforce minimum wages, and the promotion of decent work, were more effective at reducing poverty in Brazil than *Bolsa Família*.[34]

Cash transfers derive from Hayekian neoliberal logic that seeks to limit the role of the state in social provisioning and social spending. By providing cash transfers, the government limits its role and responsibilities; instead of providing basic services like water, education and healthcare it replaces those public goods with cash transfers. Crucial basic services are still in demand but inadequately provided for and cash transfers, it can be argued, let governments off the hook for not fulfilling their role to the fullest extent.

The promise of social protection and cash transfers has been based on four functions – protection, promotive, preventive and transformative.[35] Protective measures aim to provide relief from deprivation and tackle poverty and the promotive function aims to enhance the capabilities of recipients so that they can provide stability to households and enable smooth consumption. Meanwhile, the preventive function aims to prevent individuals and households from falling into further poverty.

Cash transfers are promoted as safety nets, however, due to the neoliberal nature of current global economic structures, they are unable to achieve any of these four functions effectively. Households receiving cash grants continue to live in poverty and are barely able to meet their daily needs. Studies of social policy implications and responses to COVID-19 in the Global South show how poverty levels rose following job losses and higher cost of living but even before the pandemic, poverty was surging as economies were struggling.[36] Social protection programs designed as targeted interventions could not provide security for the growing number of vulnerable people.

By targeted interventions, I mean social policies like this only reach a small group of people. In most countries, social protection coverage is limited to the poorest of the poor. In contexts where most people live below the poverty line such as Nigeria where this is true of 53% of the population and Malawi at 70.3%, cash transfers cannot create significant improvement in general wellbeing and welfare since these programmes tend to reach less than 10 per cent of the poor.[37] Instead, most of the poor end up living in destitution. Moreover, cash transfer programmes provide small amounts of money to households with most Africa-based initiatives ranging from $5 to $20. Even considering a poverty line of $1.90, the transfer amount paid is inadequate to meet the most basic of needs. The inadequate state of social services and their market price measured against a cash transfer is insufficient; despite the gift of cash the poor cannot access services.

To make meaningful contributions to poverty reduction and reduce the vulnerabilities of poor populations, governments have to institute social policy interventions that cover large numbers of people and are generous in their provision rather than relying on paltry transfers. Governments and the public would be better served by greater investment in universal programmes of health and education, and, in some cases, land reform to meet the needs of the wider population. By their nature, cash transfers are inadequate for sustainable change in African contexts that have suffered decades of state rollback in social spending.

Another inherent limit of the neoliberal ideology around cash transfers is that it atomises individuals and breaks forms of solidarity necessary for the promotion of universal welfare. Targeted transfer excludes masses of people and methods employed in targeting those who qualify alienate other community members who also live in areas of widespread poverty. Unlike universal programmes which reach whole populations, cash transfers, as they are often implemented, lack the common fabric upon which solidarity, especially class-based kinds, can be forged. Those who do not benefit from the programme see no need to advocate for larger allocations to the programme. Universal social policy programmes can also open avenues for the enhancement of national cohesion.

TRANSFORMATIVE SOCIAL POLICY AS AN EMANCIPATORY FRAMEWORK

Looking back, the post-independence period provides hope on what developmental aspirations are possible when governments make deliberate efforts to improve life for their citizens. Lessons can be learned on how universal and inclusive policies can achieve not just poverty reduction but foster national cohesion. Achievements of the post-independence period are an indication that when given space to chart their own path without interference, African governments have the capability to manage their resources through democratic policymaking processes. Though African governments may not always be perfect, they express at least on paper the will and intention to improve the lives of their citizens as a priority.

Africa today is much richer and more knowledgeable than it was at independence, with better experience of statecraft and nation building. Globalisation presents a significant challenge to navigate. As much as it was expected to bring about growth opportunities for developing countries, the embeddedness of African and Global South economies in global trade has delayed the continent's progress. Similar sentiments could be expressed with regards to social policy in Africa that has been influenced by globalisation with social policy becoming globalised. This is visible in the prominence of the MDGs and SDGs. Foreign interference and policy prescriptions that are delinked from national aspirations and lack contextual depth, can warp national processes.[38]

Transformative social policy offers a space for African countries to rethink how to respond to their needs and on how better societies can undertake production, protection, reproduction, redistribution and nation building.[39] Deriving from notions of equality and solidarity, transformative social policy focuses on structural change that goes beyond poverty reduction. Several principles are attached to the idea of transformative social policy. First, social policy can be designed in ways that bring about transformation in the economy, institutions and how people relate to each other.

Second, transformative social policy posits that social policy is more effective and able to perform the functions mentioned above if it uses multiple instruments rather than over relying on a single instrument or course of action. Most important is the interconnectedness of instruments.[40] A lack of connectedness in the social policy instruments makes them less potent. A basket of programmes identified within the transformative social policy framework including education, healthcare, agrarian reforms, labour market interventions, state-funded childcare, family and social insurance among others could go a long way in transforming society and social relations. Drawing from a wide arsenal of instruments, African governments can design social policy interventions to bring about change in the economic, social and political spheres.

For the mission of rethinking and re-making social policy in Africa, some crucial steps need to take place. African countries ought to reclaim their sovereignty in policymaking. For too long, Africa has received instructions on how to manage their affairs, what policies to institute and even how to institute them. To do this, however, they must be able to finance their own policy needs, as a reliance on foreign resources curtails sovereignty efforts. Foreign and international aid can boost government efforts to finance social policy but government expenditure provides the most stable and lasting form of financing. Beyond economic growth performance to support financing of social policies, the realisation of universal schemes that promote wellbeing depends on government's commitment towards its citizens' welfare.

ENDNOTES

1   Jìmí O. Adésínà, 'Social Policy in Sub-Saharan Africa: A Glance in the Rear-View Mirror: Social Policy in Sub-Saharan Africa,' *International Journal of Social Welfare* 18, April (2009), 38.

2   Akin Tade Aina, 'How Do We Understand Globalization and Social Policy in Africa,' in *Globalization and Social Policy in Africa*, eds. Tade Akin Aina, Chachage S. L. Chachage, and Elisabeth Annan-Yao (Dakar: Codesria, 2004), 23–46.

3   Thandika Mkandawire and Charles C. Soludo, *Our Continent, Our Future: African Perspectives on Structural Adjustment* (Trenton, New Jersey: Africa World Press, 2001).

4   Jìmí O. Adésínà, 'In Search of Inclusive Development: Introduction' in *Social Policy in Sub-Saharan African Context: In Search of Inclusive Development*, ed. Jìmí O. Adésínà (Hampshire, New York: Palgrave Macmillan, 2007), 1–53.

5   International Labour Organisation, *Social Protection Floor for a Fair and Inclusive Globalization* (Geneva, 2011), xxiii.

6   Joanne Bosworth, Carlos Alviar, Luis Corral, Benjamin Davis, Daniel Musembi et. al., 'The Cash Transfer Programme for Orphans and Vulnerable Children: The Catalyst for Cash Transfers in Kenya,' in *From Evidence to Action: The Story of Cash Transfers and Impact Evaluation in Sub Saharan Africa*, ed. Benjamin Davis, Sudhanshu Handa, Nicola Hypher, Natalia Winder Rossi, Paul Winters, and Jennifer Yablonski (New York, NY: Oxford University Press, 2016), 117–145.

7   Frank Ellis, '"We Are All Poor Here": Economic Difference, Social Divisiveness and Targeting Cash Transfers in Sub-Saharan Africa,' *Journal of Development Studies* 48 (2) (2012), 201–214.

8   Joy R.A. Otolo, Wycliffe A. Oboka and J.M. Okoth, 'Targeting of OVC Beneficiary Households in Kisumu County, Kenya,' *International Journal of Education and Research* 2 (9) (2014): 337–50.

9   Anne Schneider and Helen Ingram, 'Social Construction of Target Populations: Implications for Politics and Policy,' *American Political Science Review* 87 (2) (1993), 334–347.

10 World Bank, *Poverty and Shared Prosperity 2022: Correcting Course* (Washington, D.C., 2022).

11 UNICEF, Türkiye Earthquake Response Appeal: Humanitarian Action for Children, 1 February 2023, https://www.unicef.org/appeals/turkiye.

12 Government of Kenya, *Inua Jamii: Towards a More Effective National Safety Net for Kenya* (Nairobi, Kenya, 2016).

13 Ndangwa Noyoo, *Social Welfare in Zambia* (Lusaka: Multimedia, 2000).

14 Thandika Mkandawire, 'Social Policy and the Challenges of the Post-Adjustment Era,' in *Getting Development Right: Structural Transformation, Inclusion and Sustainability in the Post-Crisis Era*, ed. Eva Paus (New York: Palgrave Macmillan, 2013), 61–82.

15 Adésínà, 'Social Policy in Sub-Saharan Africa,' S37–51.

16 Issa G. Shivji, *Accumulation in an African Periphery: A Theoretical Framework* (Dar es Salaam, Tanzania: Mkuki na Nyota Publishers, 2009).

17 Jason Hickel, *The Divide: Global Inequality from Conquest to Free Markets* (New York: W. W. Norton & Company, 2018).

18 Said Adejumobi, 'Economic Globalization, Market Reforms and Social Welfare Services in West Africa,' in *Globalization and Social Policy in Africa*, ed. Tade Akin Aina, Chachage S. L. Chachage, and Elisabeth Annan-Yao (Dakar: Codesria, 2004).

19 Jason Hickel, *The Divide: Global Inequality from Conquest to Free Markets* (New York: W. W. Norton & Company, 2018), 33.

20 Mkandawire and Soludo, *Our Continent, Our Future*.

21 Giovanni Andrea Cornia and Richard Jolly, *Adjustment with a Human Face: Volume I: Protecting the Vulnerable and Promoting Growth* (New York: Clarendon Press, 1987).

22 Armando Barrientos and Juan Miguel Villa, 'Evaluating Antipoverty Transfer Programmes in Latin America and Sub-Saharan Africa. Better Policies? Better Politics?' *Journal of Globalization and Development* 6 (1) (2015), 147–79.

23 Sean Higgins, 'The Impact of Bolsa Família on Poverty: Does Brazil's Conditional Cash Transfer Program Have a Rural Bias?' *The Journal of Politics and Society* 23 (1) (2012), 88–125.

24 Devereux S., J. Allister McGregor, Rachel Sabates-Wheeler, 'Introduction: Social Protection for Social Justice,' *Special Issue: Social Protection for Social Justice*, Volume 42, Issue 6 (November 2011), 1–9.

25 Jason Hickel, *The Divide: Global Inequality from Conquest to Free Markets* (New York: W. W. Norton & Company, 2018), 164.

26 Friedrich Hayek, *The Road to Serfdom, The Definitive Edition: Text and Documents* (Chicago: University of Chicago Press, 2007).

27 Naomi Klein, *The Shock Doctrine: The Rise of Disaster Capitalism* (New York, NY: Metropolitan Books, 2007).

28 Daniel Stedman Jones, *Masters of the Universe: Hayek, Friedman, and the Birth of Neoliberal Politics* (Princeton, New Jersey: Princeton University Press, 2014).

29 Jìmí O. Adésínà, 'Beyond the Social Protection Paradigm: Social Policy in Africa's Development,' *Canadian Journal of Development Studies/Revue Canadienne d'études Du Développement* 32 (4) (2011), 454–470.

30 Kate Pruce and Sam Hickey, *The Politics of Promoting Social Protection in Zambia*, Effective States and Inclusive Development, Working Paper 75 (ESID Research Centre, Manchester, 2017).

31 Tom Lavers and Sam Hickey, *Investigating the Political Economy of Social Protection Expansion in Africa: At the Intersection of Transnational Ideas and Domestic Politics*, Effective States and Inclusive Development, Working Paper 47 (ESID Research Centre, Manchester, 2015).

32 Abdul-Gafaru Abdulai, *Rethinking Elite Commitment to Social Protection in Ghana: Insights from an Adapted Political Settlements Approach*, Effective States and Inclusive Development, Working Paper 112 (ESID Research Centre, Manchester, 2019).

33 Ouma, Marion and Jimi Adésínà, 'Solutions, Exclusion and Influence: Exploring Power Relations in the Adoption of Social Protection Policies in Kenya,' *Critical Social Policy* (2018), 1–20.

34 Higgins, 'The Impact of *Bolsa Família* on Poverty,' 88–125.

35 Rachel Sabates-Wheeler and Stephen Devereux, 'Social Protection for Transformation' IDS Bulletin 38(3) (2007), 23–28.

36 Tim Dorlach, 'Social Policy Responses to COVID-19 in the Global South: Evidence from 36 Countries,' *Social Policy and Society* 22(1) (2023), 94–105.

37 *World Bank: Sub-Saharan Africa Poverty Data* (World Bank, 2020) https://databankfiles.worldbank.org/public/ddpext_download/poverty/33EF03BB-9722-4AE2-ABC7-AA2972D68AFE/Global_POVEQ_SSA.pdf.

38 Marion Ouma, 'Accounting for Choices and Consequences: Examining the Political Economy of Social Policy in Africa,' in *The Palgrave Handbook of African Political Economy*, eds. Samuel Ojo Oloruntoba and Toyin Falola (Cham: Palgrave Macmillan, 2021).

39 United Nations Research Institute for Social Development (UNRISD). *Transformative Social Policy: Lessons from UNRISD Research, Research and Policy Brief* 5 (UNRISD, Geneva, 2006).

40 Adésínà, 'Beyond the Social Protection Paradigm,' 454–470.

Framing Poverty in Zambia's Neoliberal Context

Cleopas Gabriel Sambo

INTRODUCTION

Policies frame and address complex social problems, such as poverty. However, they also encapsulate distinct perspectives on these issues, influencing the way these challenges are perceived and acted upon. The narratives embedded within policies possess the power to shape the lifespan of societal challenges. Against this backdrop, this chapter examines the construction of poverty in the Zambian context and analyses narratives of poverty in welfare policy discussions.

Three key arguments are presented. First, Zambia's welfare policy constructs poverty solely in material and absolute terms, while disregarding the multidimensional nature of poverty. Second, Zambia's understanding of poverty predominantly centres on microeconomic factors, influenced by multilateral organisations such as the IMF and the World Bank. This perspective has led to a policy hegemony of depoliticised poverty. It masks the lack of political will among elites who are quick to blame the economy for continued poverty while also utilising poverty for patronage and political mobilisation during electoral campaigns. Third, the enactment of the National Social Protection Policy (NSPP) in 2014, advocating transformative anti-poverty measures as investments for growth, suggested a paradigm shift. However, my analysis reveals that the NSPP conforms to Zambia's political landscape, which has perpetuated persistent and structural poverty because it does not offer citizens entitlements due to the lack of a necessary legal framework.

CONCEPTUALISING POVERTY WITHIN THE NATIONAL FRAMEWORK

Poverty in Zambia is severe, affecting most of the population.[1] This consensus has not led to sufficient action against poverty, for several reasons. Addressing poverty requires that it be defined and measured accurately. Since action against poverty calls into question the redistribution of resources and who has the power to make these decisions, how it is understood and measured influences the actions taken to combat it. How poverty is defined 'invariably divides opinion' as chosen measures often align with the interests of specific groups. The case of Zambia illustrates how and why this occurs.[2]

Historically, poverty measurements were centered on physical survival needs, such as 'want' and 'squalor', which are akin to modern absolute poverty measures. Analysis of Zambia's Living Conditions Monitoring Survey (LCMS), the Poverty Reduction Strategy Papers (PRSPs) and the National Social Protection Policy (NSPP) shows that descriptions of poverty in Zambia primarily revolve around absolute deprivation, emphasising essentials for survival. This focus on subsistence extends to the measurement methods used in the LCMS conducted by the Zambia Statistical Agency, which serves as the basis for policymaking.

The original survey, known as the Social Dimensions of Adjustment Priority Survey, which later became the LCMS, established an official framework for conceptualising poverty in Zambia. The first survey was commissioned in 1993, and it established an absolute poverty threshold by using a food basket measure based on data from the 1991 price and income survey to identify individuals living in poverty. The 2010 LCMS survey is noteworthy, as it suggests a shift in measurement methodology in Zambia that reflects global developments.

Comparability of the Poverty Method

Issue	Past methodology	CSO methodology – LCMS 2010 report	Methodology used in CSO 'Poverty trends' publication (2009)
Food basket	Based on observed consumption patterns of households close to the poverty line (5th–6th deciles) in Priority survey 1991	Based on observed consumption patterns of households close to the poverty line (5th–6th deciles) in Priority survey 1991	**Based on observed consumption patterns of households close to the poverty line (5th–6th deciles) in LCMS 2006**
Update of poverty line over time	1991 food basket updated over time using average food CPI	1991 food basket updated over time using item specific national median prices	**2006 food basket priced using item specific national median prices**
Spatial price deflators	National price deflators used – no provincial price adjustments	National price deflators used – no provincial price adjustments	**Overall price deflator adjusted to reflect differences in prices across provinces**
Consumption aggregate Provincial deflator	Not applicable	2010 consumption aggregate expanded to include new food items captured in 2010	**1996–2006 consumption aggregates have consistent list of food items**
	Includes remittances sent	Includes remittances sent	**Excludes remittances sent**
	Includes actual rents	Includes actual and imputed housing rents	**Includes actual and imputed rents**
	Includes actual housing expenditures	Includes actual and imputed housing expenditures	**Includes actual and imputed houuosing expenditures**
Food to non-food ratios	**Use a fixed food to non-food ratio of 0.7 to 0.3**	**Ratio based on non-food share of HHs with food expenditure close to the food (extreme) poverty line. 2006 ratio is 61 to 39; 2010 ratio is 66 to 34**	**2006 ratio based on average non-food share of HHs in 5th and 6th deciles: Ratio is 58.5 to 41.5**

Figure 1. Illustration of the poverty measurement methodology from the LCMS

The LCMS declared that poverty is 'multidimensional.'[3] However, despite this pronouncement, the LCMS confines poverty to material deprivation and employs measures that are primarily income and consumption-based.

This perception of poverty displays an obsession with identifying and 'counting' people in poverty without engaging with their experiences, which tends to oversimplify their realities.[4] Despite its name, the LCMS neglects non-material aspects of daily life, such as dignity, respect, educational opportunities, and everyday social influence, which are crucial to understanding the human dimension of poverty. Defining poverty solely in terms of unmet consumption needs, leads to policy measures focused on income stabilisation rather than facilitating greater access to social services.[5] The prominence of these surveys in national discourse sets the tone of national planning.

Another concern is that this understanding of poverty neglects prevailing social norms and standards. Designing effective policies requires consideration of prevailing standards within a population, rather than solely the minimum essentials for survival.[6] This minimalist perception of poverty in Zambia naturally leads to minimalist poverty measures. The extent and nature of poverty have been underestimated. An excessive focus on the monetary cost of both food and non-food necessities in poverty measurement has resulted in distorted portrayals of where poverty occurs.[7] This recurring narrative of rural poverty, present in all surveys since 1991, is exemplified in the following excerpt from the Fifth National Development Plan (FNDP) 2006–2010:

> The preceding analysis indicates that poverty remains more severe in rural areas. The majority of rural households in Zambia depend on the consumption of their own produce. Therefore, high poverty levels in rural areas could be a result of not having adequate food by the majority of households there. The rural areas have poor infrastructure and marketing systems while labour productivity among small-scale farmers is quite low.[8]

Nonetheless, in the present framework, individuals living in poverty are categorised into two distinct groups: the 'extreme poor' and the 'moderately poor'. The extremely poor are the most severely affected individuals, including those deemed unable to meet basic minimum food requirements, even if their entire expenditure is allocated to food. Conversely, the moderately poor represent individuals who can meet their fundamental food needs but struggle to afford non-food essentials.[9][10] These classifications hold significant weight in ongoing anti-poverty programmes such as social cash transfer initiatives. Furthermore, they play a pivotal role in determining the targeting mechanisms used to identify the potential beneficiaries.[11] These classifications were consistently applied across six rounds of surveys, as illustrated in figure two.

Proportions of Zambians in Poverty

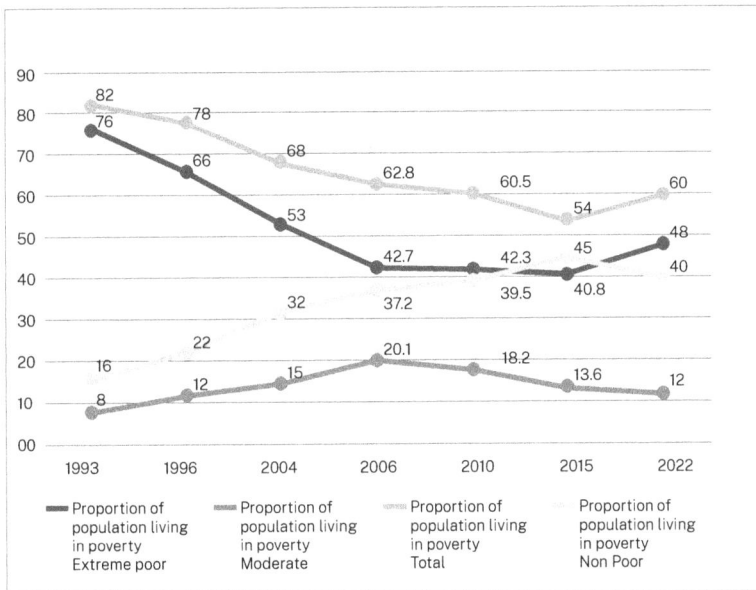

Figure 2. The proportion of the Zambian population in poverty using LMCS lines (1993–2022)

Two significant conclusions can be drawn from figure two. First, despite the constraints of the concept, poverty is an inherent characteristic of the Zambian population. Secondly, in accordance with the agency's assertion, there was a discernible positive trend, indicating a consistent and substantial reduction in the *proportion* of individuals experiencing poverty in Zambia from 1993 to 2015. This was followed by an increase from 2015 to 2022; a period during which most countries experienced setbacks due to the COVID-19 pandemic.

However, the World Bank's 2017 Monitoring Global Poverty Report argues that the ultimate concern for poverty mitigation lies in the *absolute* number of individuals residing in poverty, even though it is now customary to portray poverty proportionally within a population. Similarly, Jason Hickel, citing a shift in language from absolute numbers to proportions between the 1984 Rome Declaration and the 2000 Millennium Declaration, argues that proportions often enable the optimistic narrative of diminishing poverty levels, but are insensitive to population growth.[12] Applying this logic of absolute numbers to the Zambian case shows that poverty has been growing persistently since 1993. The number of people living in extreme poverty in 2015 was equal to the total national population in 1993. With the population of Zambia standing at 19.6 million people in 2022, there are 11.7 million people in poverty; over 8 million of whom live in rural Zambia, which has a population of slightly over 10 million people.[13] This kind of chronic intergenerational poverty is likely to drive poverty rates upwards in the future and raises questions about the effectiveness of current anti-poverty action and the usefulness of the current poverty definitions and measurements.

The political construction of poverty in Zambia has employed both structural and individualist frameworks. Frames represent the specific concepts and terminology used to present an issue, shaping both its perceived causes and its potential solutions.[14] Structural frames typically explain poverty by referencing the broader macroeconomic environment and societal structures. Conversely, individualist frames attribute poverty to individual characteristics. Policies based on structural factors often lead to comprehensive solutions, such as investments in education, skill development, and improved access to healthcare for marginalised groups. Those anchored in individualistic frames tend to propose more limited and restrictive alternatives, often emphasising dysfunction or dependency.

GROWTH FIRST: POVERTY REDUCTION STRATEGY PAPERS (PRSP) AND NATIONAL DEVELOPMENT PLANS

Zambia's PRSPs put forward a structural explanation for poverty. Their central argument was that the enduring nature of poverty was intricately linked to a deteriorating economy which had been mismanaged. This explanation foregrounded the broader economic landscape where the growth of market forces was a major priority. Politics, in this version of the events, was said to play a minor role. This framing diverted attention away from political decisions such as the allocation of state investments to specific groups and the relational dimensions of poverty, including the inequitable distribution of local economic resources and opportunities.[15] The PRSPs appeared to be growth-oriented policies whose poverty focus was the provision of basic social services and support through safety nets for highly risk-prone communities.

In what was meant to be a departure from the structural adjustment policies of the previous era, the PRSPs employed a new lexicon: 'growth with redistribution', 'broad based growth,' 'smart growth' and even 'pro-poor growth.'[16] This new lexicon was meant to justify continued reliance on PRSPs and partially conceal their reality – they were a new version of structural adjustment policies with added rhetoric sensitive to poverty. Further references to the structural causes of poverty included diseases such as HIV/AIDS, inequitable access to health, education, and income, and failure of agricultural policies. Zambia's indebtedness was identified as a barrier to prior efforts to reduce poverty. It was argued that the high national debt burden crowded out social expenditure and the absence of growth-constrained government expenditure. At times, such as in the 2002 PRSP, shortcomings in targeting and allocating resources to assist the poor and vulnerable segments of the population were mentioned.

However, the PRSPs continued to centre the marketisation logic of the structural adjustment era. The cause of poverty among small-scale farmers was diagnosed as a lack of or improper integration into the market. Individuals featured in this logic only as passive beneficiaries of economic growth. Similarly, people living in poverty were characterised as helpless victims of structural constraints, either because they could not join the formal market or because they had weak access to real assets due to unfair laws that prevented their land ownership and productivity. By analysing poverty entirely in relation to economic growth, poverty was primarily made an economic issue.

The poverty responses informed by this diagnosis primarily revolved around using macroeconomic policy to reduce poverty. The government played a regulatory role, providing essential services for individuals experiencing severe deprivation. Concurrently, it relied on efficient and effective market mechanisms to stimulate economic growth, aligning with the principles outlined in the World Bank's 1991 World Development Report. Direct interventions aimed at poor individuals included the Public Welfare Assistance Scheme (PWAS), a pre-independence social assistance programme with limited funding that targets the most destitute.[17] Additionally, fee waivers for health services in rural areas and pensioners were established. Agricultural subsidy initiatives such as the Farmer Input Support Programme (FISP) were promoted with the belief that small-scale farmers could be integrated into the credit system, thereby enhancing their economic productivity and positioning them as drivers of poverty reduction.[18]

These initiatives have overlooked the power dynamics and exclusionary relationships between these individuals and various resource networks. Status hierarchies, such as connections to influential figures or geographical remoteness, significantly impact allocation of resources within communities and between government departments. Neo Simutanyi, an expert on Zambia's political economy, argued that the state failed to consider the intricate politics of resource allocation and distribution, which extend from the heights of the ministerial level, all the way down to everyday life. Simutanyi revealed that the allocation process tends to favour constituencies represented by vocal parliamentary representatives who can negotiate effectively, or areas that are crucial for political parties to win general elections. Consequently, remote areas where more small-scale farmers reside often have fewer vocal parliamentary representatives and limited bargaining power.

During the Movement for Multiparty Democracy (MMD) government (1991–2001), for instance, the fertiliser support programme was primarily used as a reward for areas that voted for the ruling party, prioritising the delivery of farming inputs to these regions. In this approach, people in poverty were a means to political ends. Similarly, another informant, Oliver Saasa, who led the Fifth National Development Plan (FNDP) process, noted that groups such as small-scale farmers were acknowledged in the plans but, in practice, their voices did not carry the same weight as other citizens. Urban voters, who tended to be more prone to protests and perhaps whose displeasure was seen as more of an immediate threat to the state, gained more prominence. According to Saasa, national budget allocations often favoured urban projects such as infrastructure, compared to agriculture programmes aimed at benefiting small-scale farmers.

Another failing lay in the creation of the PRSPs themselves. Although claiming to be rooted in local ownership and participation and marketed as guidance documents, they were technologies of control. The emphasis on participation attempted to distinguish PRSPs from SAPs that were notoriously top-driven and implemented to disastrous results in the '90s. The PRSPs neither reversed the 'hierarchies of power' nor challenged 'institutionally produced ignorance from the top.'[19] The lack of inclusion was reflected in the inaccuracies and ineffectiveness of PRSPs.

The period leading up to the launch of the 2007 PRSP saw contradictory messages from the government regarding this growth versus poverty dichotomy. For example, the director of the Central Statistical Office, Buleti Nsemukila said:

> Our economic growth over the last two years has been nearly twice the population growth, but a growth of four per cent is not adequate to reduce poverty. We need a growth of over seven per cent.[20]

The 2007 PRSP, which became the FNDP for 2005–2010, described poverty reduction as imperative for the government. Ironically, the motivation to reduce poverty was not directly linked to livelihood and dignity concerns. Poverty was characterised as a threat to economic growth, prosperity, and political stability.

Recognising that economic growth co-existed with rising poverty and inequality, the FNDP highlighted the limitations of relying solely on economic growth for poverty reduction. This paved the way for alternative narratives on poverty in Zambia. While this was not a complete departure from trickle-down logic, it shifted the frame of discussion, in theory, to one that focused on redistribution. However, the 'important role of social protection' highlighted in the FNDP was not reflected in enacted policies or budgetary allocations.[21] Safety net type interventions such as the targeted Food Security Pack (FSP) which targeted 'vulnerable' but 'viable' farmers, and the PWAS persisted as the core of anti-poverty mechanisms.[22] There was also a donor-funded pilot social cash transfer scheme along with various agricultural subsidies.

The representation of poverty in Zambia solely as an economic issue served to normalise and depoliticise the issue. It normalised the perception that poverty could be resolved solely through technical solutions. Poverty was distanced from broader political dynamics, including Zambia's insertion in an unequal global market order. This depoliticisation also empowered the ruling elite to disassociate themselves from poverty reduction efforts, attributing poverty to global economic forces beyond their control. As a result, they could use poverty as an electoral mobilisation strategy, promising to alleviate it once in power and maintain effective clientelism.

NSPP 2014: TRANSFORMATIVE SOCIAL PROTECTION – NEW RHETORIC FOR AGE-OLD APPROACHES?

The National Social Protection Policy (NSPP) has maintained the same perspective on poverty as observed in previous policy documents. However, ideologically, the NSPP was a turning point in anti-poverty thinking in Zambia, especially in anti-poverty programming.[23] It was the first policy specifically designed to bring various anti-poverty mechanisms under one roof, an attempt at a consolidated national poverty response. The government provided a robust rationale for this consolidation:

Historically, social protection sector interventions have been implemented without a coherent and harmonized policy framework resulting in uncoordinated and fragmented efforts to reach the poor ... there has been no comprehensive and robust monitoring and evaluation system to effectively evaluate the performance of key Social Protection programmes. This has invariably perpetuated the implementation of costly yet poorly targeted and ineffective programmes that are marred with poor performance.[24][25]

By proclaiming a transformative social protection approach, the NSPP pioneered a paradigm shift from segmented safety net approaches underpinned by the trickle-down logic of the PRSP era. The NSPP also displayed the influence of a UN approach to poverty that centres dignity. It cites as its motivation the ILO's recommendation 202 for member states to develop and implement national protection floors.[26] The NSPP also problematised low budgetary allocation to poverty programmes, which had remained below 2 per cent of the national budget, mainly because social protection had been perceived as expenditure rather than investment.

The NSPP was developed and implemented by President Michael Sata who took office in 2011. Its development offers insights into policymaking dynamics in Zambia and similar contexts. Some have viewed the NSPP as a result of the alignment of global policy ideas with national progressive politics for policy reform.[27] However, Ouma and Adesina's 2018 analysis of Kenya suggested that policies like NSPP, which took root across the continent at the same time, reflected power dynamics and exclusion in the policy-making process. In these cases, international agencies influenced the policy agenda by involving experts, excluding certain local stakeholders, and depoliticising policy discussions.

In Zambia's case, Michael Sata, nicknamed the 'man of action' in his previous spells in government, had run a successful electoral campaign through populist promises of socioeconomic and political reform. These promises provide an instructive context for understanding the NSPP. Its enactment in 2014 was a noteworthy accomplishment, particularly because the MMD, the previous ruling party in Zambia for two decades, failed to create such a policy. Nevertheless, as this analysis reveals, the speed with which populist policies are developed often comes at the expense of good design, careful implementation, and fiscal and political consolidation.

For example, the NSPP defined poverty as self-perpetuating and manifesting in marginalisation, vulnerability, food insecurity and severe limitations in fulfilling basic needs. Its primary objective was to elevate households from vulnerability and poverty to resilience, increasing their capacity and food security by acquiring livelihood assets. Although it envisioned that Zambia should become a middle-income nation free from persistent or periodic critical levels of poverty, deprivation, and extreme vulnerability by 2030, it failed to offer a clear roadmap or set of indicators to achieve this vision.

NSPP interventions

The NSPP's four pillars – social assistance, social security, livelihood and empowerment, and protection – did not necessarily respond to Zambia's current poverty situation because of low coverage. Access was restricted to workers in formal employment, although efforts have been made to extend coverage to the informal sector. In 2020, only one-third of working people in Zambia were in formal employment.[28] Yet, despite pronouncements in the NSPP that a legal framework was required to harmonise social security coverage between informal and formal sectors, the status quo remains, highlighting the broader ambivalence towards true reform.

1) Social assistance and the narrative of 'incapacitated households'

The NSPP's social assistance pillar aimed to reduce extreme poverty and destitution among vulnerable and poor households, enhance food and nutrition security for vulnerable populations, and build the human capital of extremely poor households to stop the inter-generational transfer of poverty. These goals were couched in general, and not in specific terms. The NSPP planned to achieve these goals through regular transfers, strengthening connections with other social programmes, and providing disaster relief.

The mechanisms for social assistance included all the various governmental schemes previously provided for poverty relief: the PWAS and its offshoots, the Nutrition and Supplementary Feeding and Resettlement schemes, and the Social Cash Transfer (SCT) Scheme. The welfare officers implementing these programmes explained the difficulties that they have encountered:

PWAS is unpredictable. It is not like the Social Cash Transfer. With PWAS, we sometimes get funded once a year, and sometimes we get it twice. We never know when the money will come or how much it will be. It is not like the social cash transfer where you expect payment for the next two months, and so on.[29]

The social cash transfer programme has become a central focus of both domestic and international discussions regarding anti-poverty initiatives in Zambia. The government has allocated significant resources to this programme at the expense of alternative strategies, due to a form of path dependency. The programme has acquired sufficient political significance so it could potentially influence electoral outcomes, while it remains favoured among donors and cooperative partners. This preference is born of the demands of evidence-based policy making, as it is more feasible to demonstrate the impact of cash transfers targeting the ultra-poor compared to investments in the overall transformation of social services. This approach inadvertently reinforces the erroneous belief among government officials that social assistance imposes an undue burden on public finance. However, the coverage of social cash transfers employs a restrictive logic of 'deservingness' by targeting only 'incapacitated households,' with coverage remaining significantly below the number of individuals considered to be living in extreme poverty. At present, the programme reaches about 974, 160 households.[30]

2) Livelihood and empowerment for the 'vulnerable but viable'

Under the livelihood and empowerment pillar, the NSPP aimed to support households with the capacity to generate sufficient income. The interventions included providing agricultural inputs, a food security pack, a women's empowerment fund, and micro-credit facilities. However, welfare officers revealed that the same deservingness criteria used in the PRSP and the RSNDP underpinned their implementation. The livelihood interventions targeted those considered vulnerable but *viable*, distinct from the social assistance pillar, which serves the destitute poor.

Viability is often defined in economic terms, retaining the logic of productive contribution to the economy. The legacy of the PRSP logic where investment in poverty reduction was seen as expenditure, remains strong. This focus on viability continues the pejorative rhetoric of previous policies. Ultimately, the viability criterion moralises poverty and contradicts the realities of life in Zambia. For instance, it ignores gender dynamics and the experiences of women, which marks their exclusion from livelihood interventions.

The most pronounced empowerment programmes currently in operation are the Girls Education and Women's Livelihood (GEWEL) project and the food security pack, which promote human development by addressing barriers to education for girls, stimulate social and economic development through entrepreneurship among vulnerable women, and support small-scale farmers in transitioning to sustainable agriculture and food security. However, these programmes encounter several implementation challenges, including a compartmentalised approach that impedes institutional synergy, resulting in exclusions and creating gaps in resource access, thereby exacerbating the difficulties faced by individuals experiencing poverty.

After the 2021 election, the Constituency Development Fund (CDF) has emerged as the predominant empowerment programme for communities, particularly in rural regions. While the programme possesses considerable potential for community transformation, several challenges persist in undermining its efficacy. These include limited access to information among potential beneficiaries, especially in remote areas, the politicisation of the selection process, which jeopardises equitable resource distribution, and an excessively bureaucratic system that is incongruent with the lived experiences of those it is intended to assist.[31] In the absence of addressing these impediments, the CDF risks failing to fulfil its empowering mandate.

Overall, the NSPP suffers from disjointed implementation – its various programmes are implemented by different government departments without synergy. The *ad hoc* nature of the policy left it open to political manipulation. For example, a market fund for women cloaked in empowerment rhetoric was created during a political rally. Other similar programmes such as the Youth Empowerment Fund (YEP) or Presidential Empowerment Fund (PEF) were often ramped up during election periods but have been implemented without sufficient planning, monitoring and evaluation frameworks.

3) Protection

The final pillar of the NSPP, protection, attempts to transform the framework for implementing social protection mechanisms – integrating individuals equally into society, and enabling marginalised groups to assert their rights and dignity. Its guiding principles also emphasise participation, dignity, and equity. Protection emphasises Zambia's need to tackle the underlying social dynamics that create social vulnerabilities such as age, gender-based violence, orphanhood, and widowhood by strengthening citizens' legal rights. Programmes within this pillar include rehabilitation of street children, anti-violence initiatives, anti-human trafficking efforts, and legal services. This study locates the problem of poverty within its socio-political context, offering a normative and legal imperative for the provision of social protection mechanisms.

However, this policy pillar also highlights existing political contradictions. Respecting dignity requires equitable access to resources and a rights-based approach, which ensures that individuals and groups are not deprived of their inherent dignity, starting at the institutional level. However, the NSPP fails to meet the basic principles of ILO Recommendation 202, on which it is modelled. By the policy's own admission, Zambia's legislative framework lacks explicit provisions for social protection, and social and economic rights are not legally enforceable in the country.[32] This distinguishes Zambia from other countries such as South Africa, where constitutional provisions support the enforceability of such policies. In addition, the frequent use of viability criteria contradicts the dignity-focused ideals expressed.

The Patriotic Front's move to institutionalise social protection in the Constitution through a referendum was viewed as a strategic manoeuvre to secure votes in the 2016 general election. The referendum process in August of that year was marked by various technical issues. The threshold for success in the referendum was set at 50 per cent of those entitled to vote; however, the exact number of eligible voters was uncertain. The most recent national census at the time was conducted in 2010, and the next one was scheduled for 2020, so the referendum could not provide accurate population figures. While voting in the general election required a voter's card, voting in the referendum only required a national registration card, which added another layer of complexity. Moreover, the decision to pair the referendum with a general election led to a partisan divide, with the ruling Patriotic Front advocating for a Yes vote, emphasising cost-effectiveness, while opposition parties campaigned for a No vote. Civil society organisations called for the postponement of the referendum due to procedural flaws and insufficient public awareness about the referendum's purpose.[33] Consequently, the referendum ultimately failed.

However, even if the referendum had succeeded, a review of the proposed amendments reveals that the reform would have been inadequate. Article 45 of the draft Bill of Rights suggested that, while some provisions for social protection were expected, the constitutional court would still not have had the authority to intervene regarding resource allocation between the state and citizens beyond the level determined by the state. This reflects the political ambivalence, contradictions, and inconsistencies inherent in the anti-poverty efforts in Zambia. This continued absence of a legal framework undermines the human rights foundation of the NSPP, perpetuating the historical reliance on residual safety nets, rather than a truly transformative approach to poverty alleviation in Zambia. In practice, references to the rights and dignity of people in poverty become narratives of state benevolence among both policy implementors and beneficiaries.

Another weakness of the NSPP is the repeated use of ambiguous language – largely the common buzzwords of development policy. For example, vulnerability and marginalisation were key concepts frequently referenced in policy. However, marginalisation is undefined, while a generic definition of vulnerability, one that does not clarify what it means in light of the Zambian context, is given. The use of such buzzwords in policy is often a 'performance of development' giving policies a sense of 'purposiveness and optimism.'[34] The vague and ambiguous discourses enable policies to command assent from various stakeholders, while the policies' core messages pass unquestioned for how unrealistic or contradictory they are.

In the Zambian case, these vague and ambiguous discourses achieved two things – enabled the unequal power relations that sustain high levels of poverty to become institutionalised and unquestioned, while cementing the inadequate policy responses in the public pysche as the best that can be done under these circumstances. The situation has worsened due to the apparent lack of public contestation of these policy narratives in public spaces by citizens and public intellectuals alike, explained by very low national literacy, weakened labour unions and opposition political parties, and a constrained and uncritical media landscape.

CONCLUSION

This chapter critically examined the construction of poverty in Zambia within welfare policy discourses and through original interviews. From this we can see that the conceptualisation of welfare constructs poverty in an overly simplistic manner. While this approach facilitates justifying interventions that focus on smoothing consumption and tracking its progress, it fails to capture the complex social and political dynamics that not only create poverty but also aid its reproduction.

This economic-centric perspective, influenced by international financial institutions has resulted in a policy hegemony that depoliticises poverty further by obscuring underlying issues of political will. It has created fertile grounds for clientelist politicians to justify their ambivalence towards robust anti-poverty mechanisms, while exploiting poverty for political and electoral gains.

Although the 2014 enactment of the NSPP marks a paradigm shift, which advocates transformative anti-poverty investments to promote growth centre citizen dignity and entitlement, potentially charting a different path, it fails to establish entitlement-based support because of a lack of necessary legal frameworks. Effectively addressing persistent poverty in Zambia would necessitate a fundamental shift in national policy, wherein poverty reduction is pursued through deliberate and co-ordinated state interventions rather than being considered a byproduct of economic growth. This would require a transition away from the current safety net approach, which often emphasises short-term relief, instead of a more comprehensive, investment-oriented social policy framework. A new and better framework would prioritise long-term human capital development and structural reforms aimed at enhancing access to social services across all regions of the country, particularly in underserved rural areas.

A central aspect of this policy shift would be the decentralisation of governance structures, which is essential for addressing both the relational and distributional inequities between urban and rural populations. Moving beyond a 'Lusaka state' – a Lusaka-centric model of service delivery – the state must prioritise the establishment of resilient local infrastructure responsive to the specific needs of rural communities. This would also need to encompass the human and institutional capacity necessary to effectively deliver essential services such as healthcare, education, and social protection programmes. Such a system would promote greater equity in resource distribution by reducing the transactional costs of accessing services and ensuring that rural populations are not disadvantaged. Ultimately, these reforms would enable Zambia to achieve more sustainable and inclusive poverty reduction, addressing not only the symptoms but also the structural causes of inequality across the country.

ENDNOTES

1   Cleopas Gabriel Sambo, Stanfield Michelo, and Gibson Masumbu, 'Social Policy and Social Development in Zambia', in *The Oxford Handbook of the Zambian Economy* (Oxford, UK: Oxford University Press, 2024), 211; Zambia Statistics Agency, '2022 Poverty Assessment in Zambia' (Zambia Statistic Agency, August 2023), https://www.zamstats.gov.zm/wp-content/uploads/2023/09/Highlights-of-the-2022-Poverty-Assessment-in-Zambia-2023.pdf.

2   Sabina Alkire and James Foster, 'Understandings and Misunderstandings of Multidimensional Poverty Measurement', *The Journal of Economic Inequality* 9, no. 2 (2011): 289-314; Robert Walker, The Shame of Poverty (Oxford: Oxford University Press, 2014); Howard White, Tony Killick, and Steve Kayizzi-Mugerwa, *African Poverty at the Millennium: Causes, Complexities, and Challenges* (World Bank Publications, 2001).

3   Central Statistical Office, 'Living Conditions Monitoring Survey Report 2006 and 2010' (Lusaka: Central Statistical Office, 2012).

4   Ruth Lister, '"To Count for Nothing": Poverty beyond the Statistics', Journal of the British Academy 3 (2015): 139–65.

5   Martin Ravallion, 'On Multidimensional Indices of Poverty', *The Journal of Economic Inequality* 9, no. 2 (2011): 235–48; Kjell Underlid, 'Poverty and Experiences of Insecurity. A Qualitative Interview Study of 25 Long-Standing Recipients of Social Security', *International Journal of Social Welfare* 16, no. 1 (2007): 65–74, https://doi.org/10.1111/j.1468-2397.2006.00423.x.

6   Peter Townsend, *Poverty in the United Kingdom: A Survey of Household Resources and Standards of Living* (University of California Press, 1979).

7   Miniva Chibuye, 'Interrogating Urban Poverty Lines – the Case of Zambia', *Environment & Urbanization* 26, no. 1 (2014): 236–56, https://doi.org/10.1177/0956247813519047.

8   GRZ, 'Fifth National Development Plan 2005 – 2010' (Lusaka: Government Printers, 2006).

9   Central Statistical Office, 'Living Conditions Monitoring Survey Report' (Lusaka: Government of the Republic of Zambia, 2004).

10 Central Statistical Office.

11 By the eligibility criteria of the social cash transfer, least 40 percent of the Zambian population would qualify for support given the poverty head count shown in figure 2 but the programme has additional proxy means testing, which disqualifies even some of the households in the extreme poor category.

12 Jason Hickel, 'The True Extent of Global Poverty and Hunger: Questioning the Good News Narrative of the Millennium Development Goals', *Third World Quarterly* 37, no. 5 (3 May 2016): 749–67, https://doi.org/10.1080/01436597.2015.1109439.

13 Zambia Statistics Agency, '2022 Living Conditions Monitoring Survey Report', 2023, https://www.zamstats.gov.zm/wp-content/uploads/2024/07/2022-LCMS-Report-2022.pdf.

14 Shanto Iyengar, 'Framing Responsibility for Political Issues', *The Annals of the American Academy of Political and Social Science*, 1996, 59–70.

15 Maia Green, 'Representing Poverty and Attacking Representations: Perspectives on Poverty from Social Anthropology', *The Journal of Development Studies* 42, no. 7 (2006): 1108–29; Tania Murray Li, *The Will to Improve: Governmentality, Development, and the Practice of Politics* (Durham & London: Duke University Press, 2007).

16 Oliver S. Saasa and Jerker Carlsson, *Aid and Poverty Reduction in Zambia: Mission Unaccomplished* (Nordic Africa Institute, 2002).

17 Administered by the Department of Social Welfare in the Ministry of Community Development and Social Services, PWAS offers educational assistance to 'needy but high-achieving' children. It also provides supplementary nutrition to infants whose mothers have passed away. Social welfare officers explained that the programme faces limitations such as a meagre budget allocation, irregular disbursements to district offices, and discretionary allocation of support, usually prioritising a select few cases deemed urgent at the time.

18 FISP takes up 90 per cent of available government funding for agriculture and aims to support 'vulnerable but viable' farmers, but studies show that it excludes households most in need.

19 David Mosse, 'A Relational Approach to Durable Poverty, Inequality and Power', *The Journal of Development Studies* 46, no. 7 (1 August 2010): 1156–78, https://doi.org/10.1080/00220388.2010.487095.

20 Larry Monze, 'Economic Growth Rate Not Enough to Reduce Poverty – Nsemukila.', *The Post*, 9 November 2004.

21 Cleopas Sambo, 'A Relational Analysis of Poverty as a Social Phenomenon' (University of Oxford, 2018).

22 Ndangwa Noyoo, *Social Policy and Human Development in Zambia* (Lusaka: UNZA Press, 2008).

23 Sambo, 'A Relational Analysis of Poverty as a Social Phenomenon'.

24 Cecile Cherrier, 'The Expansion of Basic Social Protection in Low-Income Countries: An Analysis of Foreign Aid Actors' Role in the Emergence of Social Transfers in Sub-Saharan Africa' (Maastricht University, 2016); Marion Ouma and Jimi Adésínà, 'Solutions, Exclusion and Influence: Exploring Power Relations in the Adoption of Social Protection Policies in Kenya', *Critical Social Policy* 39, no. 3 (2019): 376–95.

25 GRZ, 'National Social Protection Policy' (Lusaka: Government Printers, 2014).

26 The recommendation is a set of principles including the overall and primary responsibility of states to provide social protection floors using a rights-based approach informed by entitlements prescribed by national law, for universal and progressive realisation using principles of dignity, equality and non-discrimination among others. The ILO Social Protection Floors Recommendation, 2012 (No. 202) (International Labour Organisation, 2012).

27 Stanfield Michelo, 'Social Cash Transfer Scale-up for Zambia', *One Pager*, no. 287 (2015), http://www.ipc-undp.org/pub/eng/OP287_Social_Cash_; Ouma and Adésínà, 'Solutions, Exclusion and Influence: Exploring Power Relations in the Adoption of Social Protection Policies in Kenya'.

28 According to the National Labour Force Survey, only 1,000, 594 people were formally employed in 2020.

29 Interview with Social Welfare Officer. MCDSS

30 Ministry of Community Development, 'Social Cash Transfer Fact Sheet', Fact Sheet, 2023, https://www.mcdss.gov.zm/?wpfb_dl=67.

31 A Money et al., 'Mobilising Investment for Climate-Compatible Growth through Zambia's Constituency Development Fund. Climate Compatible Growth Programme', 2023.

32 GRZ, 'National Social Protection Policy'.

33 NGOCC, 'NGOCC Position on the Failed National Referendum', Online (Lusaka: NGOCC, 2016).

34 Andrea Cornwall and Karen Brock, 'What Do Buzzwords Do for Development Policy? A Critical Look at "Participation", "Empowerment" and "Poverty Reduction"', *Third World Quarterly* 26, no. 7 (1 October 2005): 1043–60, https://doi.org/10.1080/01436590500235603; Deborah Eade, 'Preface', in *Deconstructing Development Discourse: Buzzwords and Fuzzwords*, ed. Andrea Cornwall and Deborah Eade (Rugby: Practical Action Publishing Ltd, 2010), vii–xi.

Monetary Policy for Africa

Redge Nkosi

INTRODUCTION

The phenomenal economic growth of East Asia, i.e., Japan, Singapore, South Korea and Taiwan from the late 1950s–1980s and later China attracted considerable attention in both research and policy circles. Instead of following the Washington Consensus or World Bank and IMF macroeconomic policy advice of deregulation, privatisation, capital account liberalisation and so on, East Asian nations were decidedly interventionist. They relied on domestic bank-based financial systems, state-owned enterprises, credit allocation schemes and other practices that run counter to so-called 'best practice.'[1]

A 2016 article on Japan summed it up nicely when it said that Japan's economic experience was 'a laboratory where theories of mainstream economics go to die'.[2] Indeed, East Asia's economic miracle has been a graveyard for conventional macroeconomic policies, the type of policies advocated by the international financial institutions. On such policies, Lord Adair Turner, former chairman of the British Financial Services Authority remarked,

> If China had more comprehensively embraced the policy prescriptions implied by the Washington Consensus over the last 10 or 20 years, its economic growth would have been considerably slower. The economic theories that underpinned those prescriptions must reckon with that fact and with China's likely continued success.[3]

Not only did East Asia's economic success provide an empirical challenge to neoclassical economics, it also simultaneously provided an alternative economic paradigm whose factual record is unimpeachable. Industrial latecomer Germany is one of the major nations to have defied the conventional approach to economic development. For these nations, monetary policy was the true servant of national development, not the markets.

On the other hand, Africa, which has been the unquestioning receiver and endless pupil of the IMF and World Bank's orthodox economic policies touted to bring about prosperity and industrial advancement, has little to show for them since the 1950s. The stranglehold of these 'best practice' policy prescriptions on Africa has been shocking, manifesting itself in the continued net transfer of financial flows to the Global North, high debt and macroeconomic instability. Yet not even the crushing misery of life for the masses on the continent has dampened the enthusiasm for these policies nor has it prompted hard questions about the continued use of the IMF and World Bank driven policy.

The view of these international institutions is that the blame for Africa's lack of economic success falls on the continent's weak institutions and lack of adequate reforms. However, with the 2007/8 financial crisis and its aftermath, it became clear, even to the Bretton Woods institutions, that the intellectual edifice of the past 50 years of mainstream macroeconomics was built on a set of well-constructed myths. Many myths, especially about money, banking and monetary policy, still obstruct the continent from clearly understanding economic phenomena and devising appropriate policy responses to Africa's challenges. Even after this failed long-running experiment with orthodox economics, Africa seems determined to learn nothing from its devastation.

Africa's adopted policy positions such as interest rate policy and the savings-to-investment nexus, have had deleterious effects on the continent. These concepts have their roots in neoclassical thought and its related variants, new classical and new Keynesian macroeconomics. Macro-monetary economists and policymakers coalesced around the belief that money is neither important for economic activity nor essential for determining the price level. Yet, at the height of this support for moneyless and bankless models, East Asia was pursuing exactly the opposite. East Asians saw money and therefore banks as profoundly important for economic activity and that these occupied an inviolable role in determining prices.

The lack of roles for money and banks in mainstream macroeconomics is central to understanding economic challenges in Africa but also critical to understanding the differences between nations that shunned the neoclassical doctrine and those that followed it. Though some mainstream economists and policymakers on the continent now begrudgingly see some role for money in their economies, they are yet to accept that banks have a profoundly important macroeconomic role to play.

This chapter seeks to contribute to the construction of a monetary policy framework that cuts across the varied African economic landscape and beyond, but is nested within a theoretical paradigm that has been empirically supported in many parts of the world. Beyond its cyclical policy application, this chapter will also show that monetary policy can be a key tool for reallocating resources towards Africa's societies of choice, such as moving towards an ecologically balanced state without venturing into the 'no growth' or 'beyond growth' fads of our contemporary world.

In constructing the key pillars of Africa's monetary policy framework, the following sections will look at the evolution of the post-colonial monetary order for Africa together with the theory and practice of monetary policy. Next, I will explore the effectiveness of the current monetary policy regime for Africa's economies and then conclude by proposing an appropriate monetary policy approach consistent with Africa's diversity and challenges.

THE THEORY AND PRACTICE OF MONETARY POLICY IN AFRICA

The current dominant monetary policy regimes in Africa, though varied, are generally orthodox. They trace their journey to orthodoxy from turbulent experiences with money and prices, fiscal dominance and debt but also the overbearing influence of colonialists and their institutions.

The institutional arrangements for monetary policy in post-colonial Africa evolved away from their inherited rules-based, open fixed exchange rate frameworks to diverse regimes intended to serve the development agendas of the newly independent states. The choice for monetary policy frameworks was informed by a range of factors including the interests of former colonial powers, developmental, ideological considerations and the intellectual fervour of the time. As such the macroeconomic outcomes, in terms of performance, stability or instability, differed markedly. Monetary policy objectives included one or a combination of any of the following: economic growth, employment, price stability and in some rare cases the stability of long-term interest rates.[4]

While many countries adopted sovereign currencies immediately after independence, some were, and still are, tied to monetary arrangements that afford them little in the way of monetary sovereignty such as those in the CFA Franc zone in parts of Central and West Africa. There was and continues to be little effective control over money as a tool of policy and full power to pursue development. Unlike in East Asia and Germany where monetary policy was a servant of national development, in Africa, current monetary policy is too light to do the heavy lifting necessary for structural transformation.

Though diverse, Africa's immediate post-independence monetary arrangements can be summarised into three broad categories: rules-based, directed and discretionary. Among the rules-based monetary policy systems include currency board arrangements and currency unions typified by the two CFA Franc zones. Some Southern African countries peg their currencies to the South African Rand in the Rand Monetary Union.

Unlike typical currency boards, the central banks in the two CFA Franc zones can lend to the government subject to statutory limitations. State-owned enterprises (SOEs) can also borrow from commercial banks which in turn could receive loans from the two central banks. Pegged to the Euro (previously to the French Franc) the two banks also have facilities at the French Treasury. The use of discretion by monetary authorities is severely limited and as such, faced with economic shocks, these monetary arrangements are unlikely to respond meaningfully.

The second group of economies, under the directed category, are those that had no faith in the neoclassical notion of 'free markets', thus required some form of control or guidance. Rationing and use of administrative controls were put in place. Prices or quantities were rationed and, therefore, prices and foreign exchange controls formed a key plank of their macroeconomic policy. Within this group are those that went the 'credit ceiling route', a form of control that directs credit for developmental or other purposes. Outside of Angola, Ghana, Guinea, Mozambique, and Tanzania which practised rationing, including controlling prices or exchange rates, this monetary regime was well established in the industrial world where the degrees of control differed, including in the UK.

The last monetary arrangement was the discretionary monetary policy regime. It featured some elements of the former two but with central banks assuming 'free markets' and the full suite of central bank policy activities were embraced. While this regime is more popular today, it is best exemplified by South Africa and its "satellite countries" (Eswatini, Lesotho and Namibia) within the Rand Monetary Area. Output and inflation have been noted to be unstable in this regime and may explain the rather unimpressive macroeconomic performance in those economies that embraced this monetary policy framework.

This diversity in monetary regimes along with challenging conditions on the ground, especially fiscal imbalances and high interest rates, created fertile ground for global finance with the aid of the IMF and the World Bank, on behalf of colonial powers, to unify monetary regimes in many parts of Africa. These external forces were responsible for the shift of monetary policy regimes in Africa towards what we now see as the interest rate policy. Even though some parts of Africa, especially West and Central Africa are pegged to the euro, the Eurozone itself is an interest policy regime to which these regions of Africa are fixed. A short history of the theories behind interest rate policy, debates on its efficacy and its suitability for Africa's development agenda follows.

THEORY AND PRACTICE: THE PARADIGM

Though diverse, the intellectual bedrock upon which African monetary policy regimes were constructed at the time, was classical theory. Neoclassical economics was finding its feet in the 1950s but quickly supplanted classical theory. In the classical theory of interest, the rate of interest is determined by saving and investment. The theory says the relationship between saving and investment is one of equilibrium between real resources: savings are equal to investment. However, this equality arises through the rate of interest equilibrating (or making equal) the supply of and demand for savings. On the other hand, the Loanable Funds Theory (LFT), advanced by neoclassical economists, is a variant of the classical theory of interest. It preserves the importance of savings and investment but departs from the classical conception of real resources and a real rate of interest to a monetary rate determined by monetary factors.[5]

On the other hand, Keynes' Liquidity Preference Theory (LPT), whose key elements are important for Africa's monetary positioning, posits that at the discretion of the monetary authorities, the long-term rate of interest can be modulated (so increased or reduced). This dimension of guidance was and is important for Africa, where high interest rates are the norm rather than the exception. The authorities' control over money also informed some African states' monetary policy regimes at independence.

The practical implementation of Keynes' LPT manifested itself in low rates of interest, lasting close to a quarter of a century both in the US and the UK and significantly aiding the two countries' post-war recovery. This policy was augmented with exchange controls and what was then called the quantitative controls of bank credit, also known as credit guidance. As I show in the final section, by guiding credit, officials would essentially be embracing the notion of disequilibrium (a lack of equality between demand and supply), thus rejecting the notion of money and credit being subject to market forces. Upon change of government in the UK, the restoration of monetary conservativism was complete, and the interest rate policy (bank rate policy) dominated instead of Keynes' monetary theory.

Inflationary pressures caused by the Korean War (1950–1953) were used by the authorities to lobby for the interest rate policy. Thereafter, a return to the classical rate of interest, which later became the neoclassical's LFT, was to be the favoured policy for years to come. In Africa, especially in English-speaking economies, economists would become highly wedded to this policy stance with devastating consequences for the prospects of African development.

Keynes' repudiation of the classical and neoclassical theory rested on two grounds: (a) that there is no constraint on the availability of money or credit, as banks create it without cost upon demand from creditworthy clients, and (b), that aggregate saving is determined by aggregate investment. The distinction between Keynes' theory and classical/neoclassical theory is important.

Unfortunately, to date, money/credit is deemed scarce in Africa and the absence of savings is viewed as the binding constraint for development. By extension, these result in high interest rates, high debts, inflation and related macroeconomic challenges. The core of Africa's monetary policy and policy challenges revolve around this misguided monetary thinking.

Once one recognises there is no constraint to the availability of money and no need to look for savings to invest, African economies would be freed from the yoke of financing for development dependent on foreign savings and high interest rates which are set up to attract such foreign money. The attendant debt build-up is also eliminated.

A lack of restrictions on the availability of money for investment was, however, business as usual in Germany, Japan, South Korea, Taiwan, and China today. However, due to the imperial influence of the LFT doctrine among post-colonial African states, aggregate investment was always deemed to be determined by aggregate savings, not vice-versa. This view has remained persistent across the continent to the present day. It follows from this view that interest rates are therefore market determined, contradicting Keynes' view that rates are a policy variable that can be altered as needed. While wedded to neoclassical theory, Africa missed the most glaringly clear monetary development in East Asia: banking. In newly independent and developing Asian countries, their banking systems were not only under state control, many banks proliferated and more importantly, the deposit-creating bank loan (bank credit) was the central cog in financing investment without any form of prior savings.[6]

During the African independence wave of the 1960s, it coincided with yet another macroeconomic development of seismic proportions which Africa has remained married to: the abandonment of full employment as a major goal of policy in favour of the adoption of growth. By about 1961, the shift away from Keynes' monetary theory was complete and gradually policy tilted towards growth away from full employment. In Global North countries, immediately upon its creation, the Organisation for Economic Cooperation and Development (OECD) set a growth target of 50 per cent for the entirety of the 1960s and on 12 September 1961 this was accompanied by the adoption of a 'Code for the Liberalisation of Capital Movements.'[7] Theoretically, these implied that the mathematical apparatus of decomposing and analysing growth into productivity, changes in labour input and the associated link to wages became the standing vocabulary of economic policy. This growth mantra and the underpinning frameworks, unlike the East Asians who preferred to ignore them, took most African economies by storm.

Consistent with this framework is that successful economic growth should be based on productivity development, an argument economist Paul Krugman and many others made, predicting the imminent collapse of East Asia, including Singapore.[8] However, reality strongly contradicted this simplification, pointing to the source of economic growth as largely elsewhere, and thus relegating productivity to the fringes. Empirical evidence *against* productivity as the primary source of growth has since grown. Despite this, for African policymakers and many other observers, productivity remains the most important source of economic growth and advancement. I will revisit the productivity issue later in this chapter.

On the academic front, the abandonment of full employment suddenly blended with the monetarist assault on Keynesianism in the 1960 and 1970s, led by Milton Friedman. His adage, 'Inflation is always and everywhere a monetary phenomenon' and the associated line of thought was highly influential on monetary policy, with central bankers making fighting inflation their primary responsibility.[9] Friedman's adage implied that newly independent African states should stay away from deploying money as a tool for development for fear of inflation.

From the 1990s, using short-term rates to control inflation would become an important macroeconomic development and its impact on Africa and other developing nations that have adopted it has been profound. Its effects have prompted many institutions, including the ILO and UNCTAD, to issue warnings against it. Despite the warnings, institutions such as the IMF and the World Bank encourage African countries to use inflation targeting as a framework with interest rates as the primary tool.

IS INTEREST RATE POLICY AN EFFECTIVE MONETARY POLICY?

With money declared to be neutral (meaning without force) by classical and neoclassical economics, the interest rate becomes the primary macroeconomic variable for growth. The interest rate policy is essentially the current monetary policy of choice for many countries including those in Africa. By manipulating interest rates, both economic activity (output) and inflation are affected, as is the policy rate (or overnight rate), which affects the whole structure of interest rates in the economy (both risky and risk-free rates). These, in turn, affect aggregate demand which is how monetary policy is transmitted into the wider economy. Two monetary policy pathways – the quantity policy and the interest policy – converge via the interest rate channel. This strategy is also said to ensure that inflation remains stable. By this reasoning, the economy is automatically held on a steady development path by the interest rate mechanism. However, the evidence does not support these conclusions.

One crucial underlying assumption of this monetary policy is that markets, especially credit markets, clear. Market clearing in economics implies that supply is equal to demand, sometimes referred to as equilibrium. Without the assumption of equilibrium, the notion of interest rates as central collapses. In reality however, there are no markets that clear, credit markets being a key example.

On inflation, the use of the interest rate policy is often justified by the need to fight inflation. Within this argument is the assumption that inflation is demand driven. While there is little controversy that demand plays some role in the inflation process, inflation is essentially a supply-side phenomenon, largely arising from the conflict between owners of capital and workers over their respective shares of income. The cost of fighting supply-side forces with demand side instruments, such as the interest rate, is tortuous for developing economies that have few countermeasures to alleviate pain.

Moreover, the interest rate policy is asymmetrical. As experiences from Europe, US, Japan and other countries show, on their own, low or extremely low rates have little impact on investment decisions and have failed to engineer any recovery or promote growth. Meanwhile, high rates can have painful consequences on debt and can add such high costs to the economy that may bring it to the brink of a recession. High interest rates can help bring down inflation but at a high cost, the sacrifice being economic output and thus employment.[10][11] The asymmetric nature of an interest rate-based monetary policy makes it a blunt instrument and Africa's continued use of this policy can only serve to generate macroeconomic challenges.

THE PRACTICAL IMPLICATIONS OF INTEREST RATE POLICY AND AFRICA

Contemporary monetary policy in Africa has three channels: interest rate, exchange rate and credit channels. The interest rate channel is popular in Africa as a transmission mechanism for monetary policy for most countries, especially for the more economically advanced countries that anchor regional growth such as Ghana, Egypt, Mauritius, Morocco, Nigeria and South Africa.

Africa has the highest interest rates of all global regions, in part due to the concentration of banking systems but largely due to the dominant monetary policy regime: the interest rate policy. The drivers of inflation are mainly external and yet are fought with high interest rates. Central banks find themselves facing an increasingly delicate balancing act, if not an act in futility: raising interest rates to fight inflation risks choking off credit channels for investment, depressing economic activity and thus reducing incomes.

Furthermore, high rates are a major source of financial and economic instability and can perversely contribute to the very inflation they intend to fight. The possibility of generating a recession is always present with this strategy. At the same time, due to this particular framework, high rates themselves are deemed necessary to attract foreign capital, which strengthens the exchange rate while depressing exports necessary to earn foreign money. On the other hand, fiscal consolidation (or austerity) is also deemed necessary to calm the weight of high debt on domestic economic activity. This further depresses economic activity in environments which already struggle with low employment and low aggregate demand.

Africa's dilemma means that development capital must be sourced domestically. However, it should be patient capital, not short-term and predatory in character. In a context where much of the productive capacity is weak and import-dependent, interest rates are artificially kept high to attract, supposedly, much-needed foreign development capital. Instead these high rates often draw in opportunistic and short-termist investors. This is what accounts for much of the financialisation that Africa experiences alongside poor industrialisation or de-industrialisation and macroeconomic instability. Only a new framework would change this reality.

MONETARY POLICY FOR AFRICA

Theoretical Grounds

With monetary policy objectives set as maximum employment, economic growth and price stability, the next task is to elaborate a monetary policy framework for Africa capable of delivering these results but without relying on the current inadequate framework with its unrealistic assumptions.

One important starting point for a monetary policy framework is the recognition that the assumption of market clearing (i.e. equilibrium of demand and supply as earlier defined) is not realistic whether in the credit or money markets.[12] This is not only the case in Africa, but across the world. Since much of contemporary economic analysis assumes that markets clear, its recommendations have little relevance in the real world. In this case, disequilibrium economics (meaning the absence of equilibrium between demand and supply) sets in and dispenses with the price mechanism. Other assumptions associated with equilibrium economics that feature in contemporary macroeconomics such as rationality, rational expectations, perfect information and perfect competition are dispensed with here as they rarely apply in practice.

What happens in markets that do not clear is rationing. That is, scarce goods are shared among the population using criteria other than the price, as happened, for example, in Britain in the post war period. Markets are rationed and therefore prices cease to be the determining factor. In disequilibrium economics where markets are rationed, the choice between the two pathways of monetary policy – quantities and prices – is clearly marked in favour of quantities.

Instead of prices determining the outcomes for markets that clear, it is the *short-side principle* that determines rationed markets. The short-side principle says that whichever quantity of demand or supply is smaller (the 'short side') will be transacted. It is the only quantity that can be transacted. So, whichever quantity of demand or supply is smaller or shorter will determine the market outcomes, and not prices.[13] This principle can be stated differently: that when a buyer and a seller get together, whoever wants to do the least amount of business (the short side), has the power and determines the amount of business that will actually get done.

In this regard, in Africa, as in most developing countries, the notion of disequilibrium holds even greater sway than it would in other places. The presence of dominant foreign firms, foreign institutions such as banks, foreign-owned local producers and buyers, monopolistic or even oligopolistic tendencies (collusion), and neo-colonial market influences (power dynamics) dismantle any fantasy of prices as a mechanism that equilibrates supply and demand but also, fundamentally dismantles the monetary policy framework that governs such markets.

Given that Africa is wholly typified by markets that are generally rationed, the determinants and sources of growth and inflation must necessarily be sought from within a framework that embraces disequilibrium. Therefore, the key macroeconomic variable cannot be the rate of interest (price). The key macroeconomic variable must be credit (quantity) which is vital for the financing of the real economy.

Keynes' views in regard to the quantity of credit and credit as central to macroeconomic analysis is captured by Geoff Tilly: 'On monetary policy, Keynes continued to argue...that [the] Bank rate [a type of interest rate] was obsolete as an instrument of macroeconomic policy management and preferred the "quantitative regulation of the basis of credit."'[14] Implied in this view is that banks have a macroeconomic role to play, yet this is unrecognised in contemporary theory. More importantly for Africa, if the money creation capacity of domestic credit by local banks were unlocked the continent would not have to rely on foreign money for development.

The primary difference between Africa on the one hand and East Asia and Germany on the other was the full recognition by the latter group that the state, by harnessing allocative powers, can engineer, over a long time, economic growth, stability and employment, but also that state commercial banking can be at the centre of bank credit creation and their directed lending could alter the economic landscape in the direction of industrial development.

Monetary Policy and Inflation

Discussions about inflation in contemporary theory revolve around the fictitious world of market clearing and related phantom assumptions. Additionally, the current dominant approach in equilibrium economics justifies using interest rates to modulate economic activity to achieve a given inflation and it assumes that inflation is demand determined. That demand can play some role in the inflation process is not controversial, however, inflation is first and foremost a supply-side phenomenon. This view is especially more applicable in Africa and the developing world more broadly and occurs as a result of conflict (for instance, a class struggle of sorts) over the appropriate share of income.

If central banks or commercial banks can be made to create and allocate credit to productive capacity (what Keynes called 'industrial use'), say for developmental objectives such as infrastructure, industrial output, and ecological development, two critical issues will flow from this: output can be increased even at full employment without causing inflation and the potential growth rate can be lifted. Schumpeter said that productive credit creation is non-inflationary and the economies of Japan, Korea, Taiwan and now China have amply demonstrated that they can grow fast without stirring inflationary pressures.[15]

The above economies that followed a disequilibrium approach to economic management did not utilise the same credit rationing regimes. It is neither possible nor advisable that African countries seeking to apply realistic economics should follow exactly the disequilibrium regime found in Germany or Japan. Prudence demands a careful analysis of both monetary and non-monetary institutions and their geographical spread (monetary geography), including a country's industrial landscape, before designing an innovative way to maximise the desired outcomes.

For African economies, the growth of East Asia holds monumental lessons in regard to the monetary policy they followed and how that policy delivered the type of standards of living they currently enjoy. However, not all scholars share these sentiments. In a famous paper authored in 1994, economist Paul Krugman's 'The Myth of Asia's Miracle' predicted the eminent collapse of East Asia. Krugman argued that successful economic growth should be based on productivity development, which was not the case with East Asia. However, the historical record shows that Krugman's prophesy was wrong as East Asia continued and continues to defy his and other equilibrium economists' doomsday prophesies.

African economies have been subjected to these types of arguments by western advisors schooled in equilibrium economics, including the South African government's recent economic strategy, the Economic Reconstruction and Recovery Plan (ERRP) of 2020, basing the country's economic reforms on poor productivity as the primary, if not the sole measure for the source of economic growth. This approach is unlikely to profoundly impact the South African economy in the direction of growth and development.

However, East Asia's growth miracle, using disequilibrium economics, was based not on productivity increase, but on the accumulation of capital (deliberate allocation of credit to investment and labour), and East Asia's predicted collapse because of lack of productivity has yet to materialise. This theoretical simplification that economic growth is solely dependent on productivity increase goes against the evidence.

A study by Vu Minh Khuong of the National University of Singapore found that about 60 per cent of Singapore's economic growth came from capital accumulation, with 34 per cent from growth of labour inputs and the rest (only about 6 per cent) from productivity improvements.[16] In more recent research, Khuong and Jorgenson of Harvard University also show that capital accumulation and growth in labour input predominates. And as the two scholars summarised, 'The secret of the Asian growth model lies not in achieving high productivity growth but in sustaining reasonable productivity growth despite the intensive mobilization of factor inputs over extended periods.'[17]

CONCLUSION

The empirical challenges faced by contemporary monetary economics, and, therefore, the difficulties of monetary policy in Africa stem from the failure of the profession to elaborate an appropriate framework that is consistent with real-life operations of markets. The outcomes for disequilibrium and rationed markets show that credit cannot be determined by prices, rather it is determined by whichever quantity of demand or supply is smaller (the short side). The short side of the market has the allocation powers to do business and thus allocate resources irrespective of the transaction price. In the market for credit, banks determine the direction and quantity of credit.

Secondly, banks are creators and allocators of money and therefore investment does not require any form of prior savings. The economic development of Africa can proceed without the need for external financing that often comes with unnecessary debt build-up and the eventual net transfer of financial resources to the Global North.

It is in this context that Benjamin Friedman remarked,

One highly useful lesson from the crisis is that although we conventionally use the label 'monetary policy' to refer to the macroeconomic policy that central banks carry out, the way this policy works revolves around credit, not money ... In retrospect, the economics profession's focus on money—meaning various subsets of instruments on the liability side of the banking system's balance sheet in contrast to bank assets, and correspondingly the deposit assets on the public's balance sheet in contrast to the liabilities that the public issues—turns out to have been a half-century-long diversion that did not serve our profession well.[18]

ENDNOTES

1   Ha-Joon Chang, *The East Asian Development Experience: The Miracle, the Crisis and the Future* (London: Zed Books, 2006).

2   Noah Smith, 'An Economics Lab Where Theories Go to Die,' *Bloomberg*, 11 March 2016, https://www.bloomberg.com/opinion/articles/2016-03-10/an-economics-laboratory-where-theories-go-to-die.

3   Adair Turner, 'China vs. the Washington Consensus,' *Project Syndicate*, 23 October 2017, https://www.project-syndicate.org/commentary/china-versus-washington-consensus-by-adair-turner-2017-10.

4   *Monetary Policy in Sub-Saharan Africa*, eds. Andrew Berg and Rafael Portillo (Oxford: Oxford University Press, 2018).

5   Geoff Tilly, *Keynes' General Theory, the Rate of Interest and Keynesian Economics* (London: Palgrave Macmillan, 2007).

6   Joseph A. Schumpeter, *History of Economic Analysis* (New York: Oxford University Press, 1954).

7   OECD Codes of Liberalisation: Users Guide: https://www.oecd.org/content/dam/oecd/en/topics/policy-issues/investment/oecd-codes-of-liberalisation-users-guide.pdf.

8   Paul Krugman, 'The Myth of Asia's Miracle,' *Foreign Affairs* Vol. 73, No. 6 (Nov–Dec 1994), 62–78.

9   Milton Friedman, 1982. Monetary Policy: Theory and Practice: A Reply. Journal of money, Credit and Banking. Blackwell Publishing, vol. 14(3), pages 404–406, August.

10 Marc Lavoie, *Post-Keynesian Economics: New Foundations* (Cheltenham: Edward Elgar, 2014), 235.

11 Richard Werner, *The New Paradigm in Macroeconomics: Solving the Riddle of Japanese Macroeconomic Performance* (London: Palgrave Macmillan, 2005).

12 Werner, *The New Paradigm in Macroeconomics*, 2005.

13 Werner, *The New Paradigm in Macroeconomics*, 2005.

14 Geoff Tilly, *Keynes' General Theory, the Rate of Interest and Keynesian' Economics* (London: Palgrave Macmillan, 2007).

15 Schumpeter, J.A., 1994 [1954]. *History of Economic Analysis*. Oxford University Press, New York.

16 Dale W. Jorgenson and Vu Ming M. Khuong, 'Potential Growth of the World Economy,' *Journal of Policy Modeling*, Vol. 32, No. 5, 2010.

17 Jorgenson and Khuong, 'Potential Growth of the World Economy.'

18 Benjamin Friedman, 'Monetary Policy, Fiscal Policy, and the Efficiency of Our Financial System: Lessons from the Financial Crisis,' *International Journal of Central Banking*, Vol. 8, No. S1 (2012): 301–309.

'Live as African': The Relevance of Thomas Sankara's Agenda for Economic Liberation[1]

Ndongo Samba Sylla

Captain Thomas Sankara, born in 1949, came to power in 1983 following a military coup organised by his comrades-in-arms. He renamed Upper Volta, the name given to his country by France, its former coloniser, Burkina Faso, which means 'land of men of integrity.' During his four years in power, Sankara tried to transform a poor and landlocked country under the yoke of French imperialist rule. The image he left to us is of a sober and honest pan-Africanist political leader. Despite his status as head of state, he kept his captain's salary, which was lower than his wife's, who was a civil servant. To assume their duty, members of his government were obliged to publicly declare their assets from 1986 onwards, 27 years before the same measure was implemented in France.

In retrospect, Sankara can be considered as a pioneering alter-globalist activist. He was concerned with ecological sustainability and was a sincere advocate of women's rights. He also advocated for the abolition of Third World countries' debt, namely in his most famous speech delivered on 29 July 1987 at the Organisation of African Unity (OAU). On that day, with eloquence, humor, and passion, Sankara pleaded urgently for African peoples to unite to face their common challenges. In particular, he called on his peers to collectively repudiate the continent's external debt, arguing that it was illegitimate owing to its colonial origins and should not be repaid. Another reason for its repudiation was that Europe owed Africa a blood debt which had not yet given rise to reparations.

However, in a stroke of dramatic irony, Sankara tragically warned, '[I]f Burkina Faso stands alone in refusing to pay, I will not be here for the next conference!'[2]

A few months later, on 15 October 1987, he was assassinated by a commando on the orders of his comrade Blaise Compaoré, who would succeed him. Compaoré, with the support of France, ruled Burkina Faso with an iron fist until his overthrow by a popular movement in 2014. He was exfiltrated in extremis by France to Côte d'Ivoire. In 2022, at a long-awaited trial, the Burkinabe justice system was able to shed light on the circumstances of Sankara's death and sentenced the absentee Compaoré and his accomplices to life imprisonment. This judgment was a hard-won victory for Sankara's family and the activists who campaigned for more than three decades for the trial.

Sankara articulated important views about African development, and more generally about economic liberation, that we can build on in our current efforts to create sustainable prosperity for nearly 1.3 billion Africans in a context marked by climate change and growing environmental stress. Here, I reflect on the relevance and current potential of the agenda of economic liberation he advocated. I elaborate on his 1987 speech given at the OAU, one of the most important speeches ever delivered by an African leader. The Zambian President Kenneth Kaunda, the chair of that year's summit, was truly impressed by Sankara's charisma, boldness, and generous pan-African vision. It is said that Kaunda told him on that day, 'I want you as the President of my country,' which genuinely reflected a deep sense of admiration, trust, and hope from the statesman 21 years his senior.[3]

Indeed, that day, Sankara urged Africans to trust their inventiveness. He promoted the slogan, 'produce in Africa, transform in Africa, consume in Africa' as a way to spur local production, enlarge domestic demand for domestic products, and reduce unnecessary imports.[4] He proposed drastically reducing prestige and sumptuary spending. He opposed military spending aimed at arming Africans against each other and encouraged his peers to discuss Africa's problems within the OAU framework in place of the platforms established by the former colonial metropoles, such as the France-Africa summits.

Sankara ended his speech with significant and far-reaching words: 'I would simply say that we must accept to live as African – that is the only way to live free and dignified.'[5] The motto 'Live as African', beyond summarising Sankara's political and ethical vision, draws up an agenda for economic liberation.

AN AGENDA OF LIBERATION

Live as African as articulated by Sankara, is not racist or xenophobic, nor is it a plea for autarky or isolationism; Sankara was truly an internationalist. In the same speech, he declared: 'The popular masses of Europe are not opposed to the popular masses in Africa. Those who want to exploit Africa are those who exploit Europe, too. We have a common enemy.' Sankara had a conception of Africanness that reminds us of the Constitution of the first Haitian Republic. When Haiti gained its independence in 1804, Haitian citizenship was not defined in a racialised way. Rather, anyone who fought to liberate Haiti from the shackles of colonial domination was considered Haitian. Even the much-celebrated 1789 French Revolution did not go as far as Haiti.

Live as African is an agenda for liberation. Argentine philosopher Enrique Dussel, who wrote extensively on the philosophy and ethics of liberation, introduced the concept of critical or negative ethics. According to him, the first principle of critical ethics suggests that we must oppose 'every ethical system that entails the production of certain victims.'[6] This stance requires ethical systems to be assessed from the location of their specific victims. An agenda of economic liberation must, by definition, be articulated from the perspective of the victims of the current global economic system. It aims to resist the existing global economic order and possibly transcend it in favour of an alternative way of organising economic and political life that would empower the considerable number of victims that continue to be produced while the status quo prevails.

The Live as African motto starts from the acknowledgment that African popular masses have been and are dominated and they must end this situation themselves. The liberation of the continent will not come from outside. Africans will have to liberate themselves from the legacies of racism, colonialism, and imperialism.[7] However, this will only be possible if Africans regain trust in themselves, unite forces, and promote their material and cultural resources. Furthermore, any project of liberation must have epistemic and educational underpinnings.[8]

Live as African is a powerful expression of self-sufficiency as an ideal, self-sufficiency understood both as freedom from external domination and as capacity for self-determination. It points to the urgent need to delink from an oppressive and exploitative world economic system as a first step towards self-determination and more prosperous and egalitarian polities. During his four years as president of Burkina Faso, Sankara did his best, in adverse circumstances, to implement a policy of economic self-sufficiency based on the mobilisation of domestic resources, and fight against corruption and financial waste. Although some policy errors were made, significant socio-economic achievements were recorded.

No worthy development strategy for the African continent can do without the Live as African programme that Sankara called for. Its necessity is evident when we put Sankara in conversation with the Brazilian economist Celso Furtado (1920–2004) and the Franco-Egyptian economist Samir Amin (1931–2018), as I do in the following section. These two Global South thinkers provided the theoretical foundations for a Sankara-style economic liberation agenda by challenging the still dominant view that developing countries can replicate a Western development trajectory. Furtado and Amin concluded that our people will never be able to catch up with the average standard of living in the Global North. Since then, some empirical studies on the phenomenon of unequal ecological exchange have confirmed their prognosis and thus insisted, as Sankara did in his time, on the need for Global South alternatives to the unsustainable Western development path. Based on these considerations, I close this chapter by exploring the kind of contemporary policy that could support a Live as African program.

THE MYTH OF ECONOMIC DEVELOPMENT

Furtado is one of the most prominent intellectuals of his generation. Influenced by great thinkers such as Karl Marx, John Maynard Keynes, Joseph Schumpeter, and Raúl Prebisch, he was a pioneer of development economics and a leading figure of structuralism in Latin America. He worked at the Economic Commission for Latin America and he was the first Brazilian Minister of Planning. Before his death in 2004, he was nominated for the Nobel Prize in Economics.

In 1974, Furtado published in Portuguese a small and relatively ignored book called *The Myth of Economic Development*. The English edition was released only in 2020, on the 100th anniversary of his birth. *The Myth of Economic Development* is a prescient book that discusses, from a Global South perspective, *The Limits to Growth*, a landmark report by the Club of Rome, a best-seller in environmental literature and a source of inspiration for the current 'degrowth' movement. It analysed and projected the interrelationships and behaviour from 1900–2100 of five main factors: population, industrial production, agricultural production, natural resources, and pollution. *The Limits to Growth* arrives at the following major conclusions.

First, economic growth is not the solution to the most pressing issues humanity is facing, it is actually the big *problem*: 'That which all the world sees as the solution to its problems is in fact a cause of those problems'.[9] Second, the idea of endless economic growth in a finite world is absurd. Sooner or later, limits will be reached. Not all resources that allow for exponential growth of capital, population, industry, and agriculture are renewable. Regarding 'carbon sinks', the industrial system has irreversible consequences on the physical environment which compromise the planet's ability to withstand the increased pressure imposed on it.

Third, the pursuit of economic growth will lead to the overshoot and collapse of industrial civilisation, if the global trends observed in population growth, industrialisation, food production, pollution, and resource depletion continue. If nothing is done to reverse the trends, limits will be reached during the 21st century. *The Limits to Growth*'s conclusions echo the current message from reports regularly published by the Intergovernmental Panel on Climate Change (IPCC) of the United Nations. Last, but not least, technological progress will not help push the limits of growth. Only a radical change in the value system – production and consumption behaviours – can help prevent civilisational collapse.

As a major recommendation, the authors of the book proposed a global strategy to achieve what they called 'global equilibrium' or a 'non-growth state' (which is a state that can allow every inhabitant of the Earth to live well). They stressed that developed countries should radically adjust their lifestyles and help developing countries towards achieving global equilibrium.

Furtado saw three merits in *The Limits to Growth*. First, it modelled the world economy as a closed system. Until then, the dominant approach had been to start from individual countries and assume that non-renewable resources were unlimited in the rest of the world. Second, it addressed an overarching issue largely ignored by economists: the consequences of capital accumulation on the physical environment. Third, it showed the ecologically unsustainable character of industrial capitalism.

However, according to Furtado, *The Limits to Growth* suffered two limitations from a Global South standpoint:

- First, it obscured the great dependence of core countries (the developed/Western countries) on the natural resources of the peripheral countries (the Global South).
- Second, it also betrayed an ignorance of the specificity of underdevelopment. Indeed, *The Limits to Growth* made projections based on the questionable assumption that 'as the rest of the world develops economically, it will follow basically the US pattern of consumption'.[10]

This last assumption sums up what Furtado called the myth of economic development – the belief in economic catch-up.

In his discussion of *The Limits to Growth*, Furtado reached three major conclusions. First, the pressure on natural resources in the future will be much less than that projected by the book's authors since the consumption pattern of core countries concerns only a minority of the world's population and can never be generalised to the whole planet. In other words, pressure on global resources is attenuated by the functioning of the global economic system which prevents populations in the Global South achieving the same consumption patterns as in the Global North. He writes:

> The predominant evolutionary tendency is to exclude nine out of ten people from the principal benefits of development; and, if we observe the group of peripheral countries, in particular, we realise that there the tendency is to exclude nineteen out of twenty. This growing mass of the excluded—in absolute and relative terms—that is concentrated in peripheral countries constitutes, in itself, a heavy factor in the evolution of the system.[11]

His second conclusion is that the generalisation of the 'Western way of life' leads to the collapse of civilisation:

> *The Limits to Growth* "provides a thorough demonstration that the lifestyle created by industrial capitalism will always be the privilege of a minority. The cost of this lifestyle, in terms of the degradation of the physical world, is so high that any attempt to generalize it would inevitably lead to the collapse of an entire civilization, putting the survival of the human species at risk. *We have then thorough evidence that economic development—the idea that the poor peoples can one day enjoy the lifestyles of the currently rich peoples—is simply unattainable*. We now know incontrovertibly that peripheral economies will never be developed, in the sense of being similar to the economies that currently make up the center of the capitalist system."[12] (italics added)

His third conclusion has a more programmatic aspect: the impossibility of economic catch-up does not imply that the citizens of the Global South are condemned to suffer from poverty and inequality. It only implies that:

• Capitalism has nothing to offer as a prospect of a decent life for the vast majority of humanity.
• An alternative *orientation of development* should be devised that is more egalitarian and more economical in resource use. To

that end, priority should be given to wide social dissemination of consumer products whose production escapes the modernist cult of planned obsolescence.

WESTERN DEVELOPMENT, SURPLUS LABOUR, AND EMIGRATION

Furtado was not alone among Global South thinkers in the rejection of the economic catch-up view. Amin reached similar conclusions via a different theoretical road. The former director of the Third World Forum observed that the secular destruction of the peasantry in the Global North went hand in hand with an important growth in agricultural productivity. In 19th century Europe, industrialisation made it possible to productively employ a large part of the labour force released by the agriculture and crafts sectors. But that was not enough to absorb the surplus labour force. Emigration, especially to the Americas, provided the main outlet. Britain, the leading economic hegemon at that time, is probably the most eloquent example of this pattern. As Utsa and Prabhat Patnaik wrote in *A Theory of Imperialism*,

> Between 1821 and 1915, over 16 million persons migrated permanently out of Britain ... a number larger than Britain's 1821 population. British emigration alone made up 36 per cent of all emigration from Europe during this period. The average number of persons migrating every year from Britain over this period works out to nearly half the annual increase in population.[13]

However, if the countries of the Global South were to follow the same development trajectory as the West, this would lead to a large dispossession of peasants and thus the creation of a huge surplus labour force. However, this surplus labour force would not be absorbed by the modern sector due to the absence of industries or the capital-intensive nature of the technologies used. In contrast to 19th century Western Europe's industrialisation phase, there is no place on the planet where the Global South could export its surplus labour, composed of informal sector workers.

Despite the Western media frenzy about migrants, the fact is the Global North is rather closed to workers from the Global South, especially low-skilled ones. One of the main features of the current world system is that there is very little movement of labour, especially from the South to the North. At current emigration rates, if we were to relocate 10 per cent of the poor population from the South to the North, it would take 200 years, according to economist Branko Milanovic.[14]

Disparity in living conditions between the North and South and within the South remains the norm. Nowadays, as Amin argued,

The demands that industries in the peripheries should be "competitive" on world markets justify the use of modern technologies which reduce the level of labour-intensive work. At the same time, there are no new Americas to open for mass migrations from Asia or Africa. In such conditions, the pursuit of a model based on historical capitalism produces nothing other than migration from devastated countrysides to squalid urban slums. [15]

In a nutshell, the limited opportunities for large-scale emigration is another important reason why the countries of the Global South must find a path of their own.

UNEQUAL ECOLOGICAL EXCHANGE

In favour of the Furtado and Amin views, a growing body of evidence has shown that the Western development trajectory during the last two centuries was based on an ecological exceptionalism, or more accurately, on ecological imperialism. It rested on the net appropriation of the resources of the Global South and the externalisation to the Global South of the ecological costs of capitalist expansion. These two patterns combined render economic catch-up impossible for the Global South as a whole.

If economic catch-up were to happen, Global South citizens would have to achieve the same levels of consumption and waste as the average citizen in the Global North. Yet, we know that if all the inhabitants of the earth had the same ecological footprint as the average resident of the European Union (EU), 2.8 planets would be needed while we only have one. The EU represents only 7 per cent of the world's population, yet it uses 20 per cent of the planet's biocapacity.[16] The planet could not afford the universalisation of the unsustainable European way of life.

In January 2021, an article titled 'Global patterns of ecologically unequal exchange: Implications for sustainability in the 21st century', highlighted three empirical results of the literature on unequal ecological exchange. Firstly, developing countries lose both on flows of biophysical resources and on monetary flows: '[High income] nations accomplish a net appropriation of materials, energy, land, and labor, while simultaneously generating a monetary surplus from those net appropriations.'[17] Secondly, economic growth in developed countries depends on unequal ecological exchange – 'The economic growth of wealthier regions is achieved through high mass throughput and concurrent environmental burden shifting to poorer regions.'[18]

Third, economic catch-up for the Global South is impossible:

> Because the economic growth model of industrialisation requires the appropriation of resources from poorer regions, it seems illusory for all poorer nations to be able to 'catch-up' by – among other things – accessing even poorer regions from which to appropriate resources. Industrialisation as experienced by the world's wealthiest countries, and some emerging economies like China, cannot become universal.[19]

The question we may ask here is: *how is it possible that the Global South loses both on net biophysical resource flows and on net financial flows?*

For this situation to exist, the Global South must be structurally in a position of financial indebtedness to the Global North. This begs another question: *how can the debt be repaid to the Global North in hard currency?* The answer is permanent austerity for the majority in the Global South and the selling-off (and privatisation) of national assets. The enforcement of so-called creditors and investors' rights is ordinarily the province of the International Monetary Fund (IMF) and the World Bank whose objective role is to facilitate the drain accruing to the Global North through unequal exchange.

Sadly, unequal ecological exchange has been the story of post-independence Africa. Due to colonial inheritances of economic specialisation most African countries alternate between growth cycles stimulated by improved prices for commodities and austerity cycles marked by declining terms of trade and debt distress.

For example, the 1960s were a decade of relatively high economic growth on average for sub-Saharan Africa. In the following decade, the average rate of growth declined due to deteriorating terms of trade. But foreign currency debt, as a ratio of GDP, increased. Issuance of foreign currency debt tends to increase with investors' confidence in brighter growth prospects. Unfortunately, worsening terms of trade and higher borrowing costs paved the way for a debt crisis that the IMF and World Bank managed from a creditor perspective. As a result, many African countries experienced lost decades in terms of real GDP per capita growth. Yet, their foreign currency debt/GDP ratio continued to increase, a clear sign that austerity policies are not designed to help countries recover economically and achieve a better financial position. Rather, austerity policies are designed to punish countries and put them at the mercy of their creditors.

The foreign currency debt/GDP ratio declined only with the partial cancellation of bilateral and multilateral debts from the first decade of the 2000s. Growth resumed, even if it was jobless. Thanks to more peaceful political climates and improved terms of trade, sub-Saharan Africa recorded its best decade of performance, prompting the 'Africa rising' narrative. Investors' confidence was back. However, with the end of the super commodity boom cycle in the beginning of the 2010s, economic growth slowed down. It was sustained mostly through onerous infrastructure projects sometimes financed by the issuance of debts in foreign currency. Foreign currency debt stock had been gradually reconstituted (see Figure 1). The COVID-19 pandemic would just expose further the unsustainable foreign debt trajectory of a number of African countries. The pandemic did not create the debt distress, it just accelerated it, given that all the debt sustainability indicators have been deteriorating from 2008.

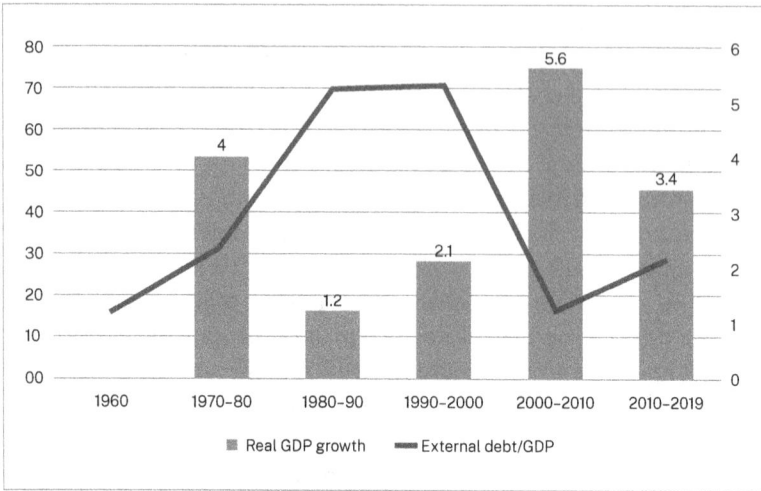

Figure 1: Evolution of the average real GDP growth and the external debt/GDP ratio for sub-Saharan Africa (1960–2019) (in percentage)[20]

In grey, right scale, we have the average real GDP growth per decade; the line, left scale, corresponds to the external debt/GDP ratio at the beginning of each decade. The graph contains data for 30 countries for which data are complete for the whole period. Average real GDP growth by decade is provided for the period from 1970.

One thing Sankara understood, which is not yet clear to most progressive intellectuals and movements, is that cancelling existing foreign currency public debt is far from enough. While discussions about the need to find an international and functional mechanism for sovereign debt restructuring are probably as well-meant as campaigns for debt cancellation or debt jubilee, they often miss the elephant in the room. Sankara knew that the system of unequal ecological exchange is what needed to be abolished first. Though important, the repudiation or cancellation of the outstanding foreign debt would not be enough.

As long as foreign debt cancellation or repudiation does not become the foundation for another development path, its benefits risk being temporary and pyrrhic. Between 2000 and 2016, for 28 countries representing 85 per cent of sub-Saharan Africa's GDP, interest paid on external debt amounted to $100 billion. Though very significant, this was five times less than the income accruing to foreign direct investment during the same period for the same sample of countries.[21][22]

Yet, there is no campaign asking to cancel the repatriation of these huge amounts of profits and dividends to pay the interest on loans, which ultimately contribute to the reconstitution of the continent's foreign debt stock.

In sum, there is logically no sustainable development for Africa and the Global South in a world of unequal ecological exchange. Even the commendable UN sustainable development goals are not sustainable in practice. They still cling to the economic catch-up view and do not acknowledge the unequal ecological and economic realities of developing countries.

DELINKING AND SELF-CENTRED DEVELOPMENT

Experimenting with another development path is a necessity and this is the basis of the delinking strategy advocated by Amin. Far from being synonymous with autarky, a delinking strategy implies instead prioritising the domestic needs of the peripheral countries over the demands of the global economic system. It means implementing policies that lead to a greater local control over (i) the reproduction of the labour force, (ii) the domestic market, (iii) natural resources, (iv) technology, and (v) the 'centralization of the economic surplus' – that is, the control over the financial system and flows and the ability to direct domestic investment.[23][24]

While Amin theorised delinking, Sankara was obliged by the circumstances of his country to experiment with a form of forced delinking. Sankara invited Amin to come to Burkina Faso to discuss the country's economic challenges. When Amin arrived Sankara said to him: 'You have told us that we must have the courage to de-connect [delink]. Before we could gather that courage, the French have taken the lead and de-connected [delinked] us. What shall we do?' As Amin recollected some years later, 'I had not imagined that the question of de-connection [delinking] would first arise in a country as poor as Burkina Faso.'[25]

Retrospectively, there were some objective limitations to Sankara's agenda of economic liberation. One was the lack of a supportive regional integration framework. A landlocked country such as Burkina Faso must leverage trade and financial ties with its neighbors. Another was the weak support of political leaders in the region, who except for the Ghanaian President Jerry Rawlings, were not especially enthusiastic about the Burkinabe revolution and its young and unconventional leader.

A further limitation was the nation's lack of monetary sovereignty coupled with the lack of understanding of the cardinal importance of money and finance. Burkina Faso is still a member of the franc zone, the last colonial monetary zone in Africa. The strategy of domestic resource mobilisation promoted by Sankara would have greater economic impact and popular support with the appropriate monetary and financial instruments. Given the little financial help received from outside, the Burkinabe revolution happened in a context of severe self-imposed austerity that was resented by the middle classes at the time. Sankara himself acknowledged that it was very tough to deeply transform an underdeveloped country when the state budget was as little as 58 billion CFA francs, with 72 per cent of it devoted to pay debt and the salaries of 30 000 civil servants.[26]

One major lesson from the Burkinabe revolution is that a strategy of domestic resource mobilisation requires a minimum in terms of monetary sovereignty to be successful over the medium and long term. Burkina Faso, under Sankara, was heavily money-constrained and this limited the scope of popular support. Yet, as Modern Monetary Theory (MMT) shows, money can never be an absolute constraint. Governments that issue their own fiat currency can never lack their own currency.[27][28] In principle, they will always be able to finance, in their own currency, any project that relies essentially on real resources available locally or that can be developed locally. In contrast to financial resources, real resources refer to land, labour, equipment, intermediary inputs, etc.

The paradigmatic revolution introduced by MMT opens up a developmental space that has been hardly explored. In contrast to the current extraverted development path that makes African countries economically vulnerable and highly dependent on foreign trade, technology, and international finance, it is possible to create sustainable prosperity that reduces external dependency in its various facets. With Live as African as the guiding spirit, this path consists of mobilising domestic resources in an institutional framework of monetary sovereignty.

By an institutional framework of monetary sovereignty, I mean an intellectual and policy framework where the following facts are acknowledged. First, a government issuing a sovereign currency can never lack money and its spending is not limited by its fiscal receipts; second, investment is not constrained by available savings; and three, real resources constraints are the ones that matter most of all.

From the 1960s to date, most calls for African self-reliance have been unaware of a different mindset towards monetary sovereignty, as they subscribe to the belief that money is a scarce resource, and relatedly, that taxes finance public spending and savings constrain investment.[29] By uniting Sankara's approach to MMT's description of the operational realities of the monetary system, we can delineate a promising approach to economic development able to deliver the basics of decent life to anyone while reducing African nations' external dependency. I would say that the challenge is MMT-ing Sankara or if we prefer Sankara-ing MMT.

AN EXAMPLE OF DOMESTIC RESOURCE MOBILISATION

To illustrate this point, let us take a concrete example from the revolutionary work being done by Diébédo Francis Kéré, a Berlin-based architect born in Burkina Faso. He recently won the prestigious Pritzker Prize 2022, which is often referred to as the Nobel Prize for Architecture. Kéré's work epitomises perfectly the Live as African approach. As a pioneer of sustainable construction, he built schools in his native village, using essentially local materials. In March 2022, following the announcement of the Pritzker Prize, he was interviewed by a French TV channel.[30] Here are some excerpts:
To the question 'What inspired you to build schools using local materials?' he replied,

> I always resented the fact that children are sitting in classrooms where it's very hot, where there's no light, in a country where there is the sunlight all day. I said to myself, we must use what is abundant to create classrooms that provide comfort for teachers and students but also classrooms that are inspirational ... I want-

ed to bring beauty to the neediest. In doing so, the techniques came. That is, how to create passive ventilation, how to create a roof that supports passive ventilation and at the same time protects the building from the weather. That's how I did it, by modernizing the earth, by adding aggregates to it … I didn't just stop there. In Burkina Faso, there is laterite. I used it by cutting it to make facades that give the feeling of modernity that inspires. I also used local wood … to create facades to protect the walls from the sun and thus create a shaded and welcoming space for the users. That's my way of doing it.[31]

To the question 'Why don't Africans use local materials, so-called traditional materials?' Kéré's reply was:

The West, by its way of doing or its way of saying that what we have is primitive and has no value, we end up rejecting what we have. This leads to saying, for example, that building with the earth is synonymous with poverty. I did not want to accept this. I wanted to improve the earth and create buildings that inspire … We have to convince people. We must not let ourselves be stopped but we must prove that what we have can be the basis for the development of our country. I did this by using earth to build my first school.[32]

When asked, 'Why should Africans go back to these materials?' he replied, 'If you continue to use materials that don't come from home, the resources will disappear. If you use what you have and take advantage of it to improve local skills, you make people proud and add recognition to what we have. That's what's going to move us forward.'[33]

From this rich interview, I derive three major lessons. First, cultural alienation has worked to diminish Africans' sense of self-esteem. Worse, it led us to devalue what we are and what we possess. Second, cultural alienation coupled with the imposition of development agendas from abroad have prevented Africans from exploring an endogenous development path that could deliver sustainable prosperity and improve self-esteem and recognition. This lack of self-determination has until now produced unnecessary suffering and hardships. Third, the quest to ground African development in domestic resources itself stimulates a process of creativity and innovation. At the same time, there is already enough creativity within the continent. Throughout Africa and its diaspora there exist people, unknown to most of us, who are achieving in their field of expertise what Kéré has achieved in the domain of architecture.

What creative minds like Kéré, policymakers must know that whatever is feasible locally from a technical and material point of view can be in principle financed in the domestic unit of account of the sovereign issuer of the currency. Sankara-ing MMT or MMT-ing Sankara consists of connecting the strategy of mobilising domestic real resources with the possibilities associated with monetary sovereignty. In other words, it consists of implementing projects based on domestic real resources and financed essentially in the national currency. This development path creates prosperity for the majority while reducing external dependency. It could be further leveraged provided that regional or continental integration is also designed according to the Live as African approach.

None of this implies that African countries do not need foreign technology or finance or international solidarity. Rather, the argument is that international co-operation and solidarity should stop being introduced *deus ex machina*. It should be tailored to meet the specific needs and constraints arising from African countries' strategies to mobilise their domestic resources. The real test for international co-operation and solidarity is to demonstrate whether it helps increase African self-reliance. For example, in place of a collaboration that creates technological dependency, a Live as African approach to international solidarity would promote co-operation to develop liberation techniques, tools, and methods that allow the continent and its inhabitants to increase their capacity to mobilise their domestic resources and lessen the reliance on foreign resources.

As Sankara rightly said, "We must accept to live as African – that is the only way to live free and dignified." It is also the only way out of the current dead-end. Humane and ecologically sustainable development must be embedded in the mobilisation of local resources. After all, as he observed, 'We have enough intellectual capacity to create or at the very least use technology and science wherever we find it.'[34] The good news is that everything that is technically feasible locally can, in principle, be financed in the domestic currency. This is the liberating message of the monetary sovereignty perspective.

So, what could an agenda of economic liberation for Africa à la Sankara look like today? It could revolve around this idea: the basic elements of a dignified life, such as food, safe water and environment, shelter, education and local transport, should be de-commodified and, wherever possible and desirable, should generally be free of charge. Neither privatisation nor oligopolistic market actors must decide the fate of peoples and nations.

This agenda should be implemented by focusing on the ecologically sustainable mobilisation of domestic, regional and continental resources. To be successful, it requires renewed forms of democratic and collective leadership, pan-African solidarity and international solidarity. This agenda for economic liberation is not a utopian vision. There is enough human, cultural, and material wealth potential on the African continent to make it happen.

ENDNOTES

1   The author would like to thank Prof. Kai Koddenbrock and Prof. Sabelo
    Ndlovu-Gatsheni for their valuable comments on a previous version of
    this chapter. In 2022, an earlier draft of this essay was presented at a
    University of Bayreuth African Studies Working Papers session.

2   Thomas Sankara, 'Thomas Sankara: A United Front Against Debt', *Progressive
    International*, 27 February 2021, https://progressive.international/
    wire/2021-02-26-thomas-sankara-a-united-front-against-debt/en.

3   Ndongo Samba Sylla, *Redécouvrir Sankara. Martyr de la Liberté* (Berlin:
    AfricAvenir/Exchange & Dialogue, 2012), 225.

4   Sankara, 'A United Front Against Debt'.

5   Sankara, 'A United Front Against Debt'.

6   Eduardo Mendieta in Enrique Dussel, *Twenty Theses on Politics* (Durham/
    London: Duke University Press, 2008), x.

7   For Sankara, transforming society away from colonial legacies and
    some oppressive 'traditions' required political education. Leadership
    by example was paramount, as well as raising people's awareness and
    sense of solidarity through the practice of subaltern experiences (for
    example, inducing men to perform tasks ordinarily reserved for women
    or introducing urban people to rural life).

    More generally, as Fidèle Toé, Sankara's childhood friend, remembered:
    'For Sankara, the question of education is fundamental. I think that we did
    not let him go to the end of his thought. Thomas would have liked us to do
    something like what they did in Cuba: take three or four years to launch a
    literacy campaign to eradicate illiteracy, put all children and young people
    in school. As a result, trained human capital could have been properly
    put to good effect. The population would have had materials to raise their
    intellectual level: everyone could read newspapers, books and participate
    in debates, write, etc. However, he built schools. That's all he did. ... Under
    Sankara, schooling made a spectacular leap (Sylla, *Redécouvrir Sankara*, 214).

8   Sabelo J. Ndlovu-Gatsheni, *Decolonization, Development and Knowledge in
    Africa: Turning Over a New Leaf* (London: Routledge, 2020).

9   Donella Hager Meadows, 'The history and conclusions of The Limits to
    Growth,' *System Dynamics Review* 23, 2/3 (2007): 191–197.

10 Donella Hager Meadows, Dennis Lynn Meadows, Jürgen Randers and
    William Wohlsen Behrens III, *The Limits to Growth: A Report for the Club of
    Rome's Project on the Predicament of Mankind* (New York: Universe Books,
    1972), 109.

11 Celso Furtado, *The Myth of Economic Development* (Newark: Polity Press,
    2020), 61.

12 Furtado, *The Myth of Economic Development*, 62.

13 Utsa and Prabhat Patnaik, *A Theory of Imperialism* (New York: Columbia University Press, 2017), 56–57.

14 Branko Milanovic, *The Haves and the Have-nots: A Brief and Idiosyncratic History of Global Inequality* (New York: Basic Books, 2010), 124.

15 Samir Amin, 'To the Memory of Sam Moyo,' *Agrarian South: Journal of Political Economy* 5, 2 & 3 (2017): 3.

16 WWF, *EU Overshoot Day Report: Living Beyond Nature's Limits*, 2019, https://www.footprintnetwork.org/content/uploads/2019/05/WWF_GFN_EU_Overshoot_Day_report.pdf.

17 Dorninger, Christian, Alf Hornborg, David J. Abson, Henrik von Wehrden, Anke Schaffartzik, Stefan Giljum, John-Oliver Engler, Robert L. Feller, Klaus Hubacek and Hanspeter Wieland, 'Global patterns of ecologically unequal exchange: Implications for sustainability in the 21st century,' *Ecological Economics* Vol. 179 (2021), 10.

18 Dorninger et. al., 'Global patterns of ecologically unequal exchange,' 10.

19 Dorninger et. al., 'Global patterns of ecologically unequal exchange,' 10.

20 World Bank, Development Indicators, July 2022, https://databank.worldbank.org/source/world-development-indicators.

21 Ingrid Harvold Kvangraven, Kai Koddenbrock and Ndongo Samba Sylla. 'Financial subordination and uneven financialization in 21st century Africa,' *Community Development Journal* 56, 1 (2021): 119–140.

22 Ndongo Samba Sylla, 'Imperialism and Global South's Debt: Insights from MMT, Ecological economics and Dependency Theory' in *Imperialism and the Political Economy of Global South's Debt*, ed. Ndongo Samba Sylla (Northampton: Edward Elgar, 2023).

23 Ingrid Harvold Kvangraven et.al., 'Financial subordination and uneven financialization in 21st century Africa,' 119–140.

24 Amin, Samir, *Delinking: Towards a Polycentric World* (London: ZED Books, 1990).

25 Mahmood Mamdani, 'Mahmood Mamdani on Marxist intellectual Samir Amin,' *Africa is a Country*, 23 December 2018, https://africasacountry.com/2018/12/mahmood-mamdani-on-marxist-intellectual-samir-amin.

26 Sylla, *Redécouvrir Sankara*, 225.

27 Warren Mosler, *Seven Deadly Innocent Frauds of Economic Policy* (Las Vegas, Valance, 2010)

28 Larry Randall Wray, *Modern Money Theory: A Primer on Macroeconomics for Sovereign Monetary Systems* (New York: Palgrave Macmillan, 2015).

29 The absence of a monetary sovereignty perspective amongst other African leaders of the time can be seen in texts such as the celebrated 1967 Arusha Declaration written by Tanzanian President Julius Nyerere. He wrote,

'When it is said that Government has no money, what does this mean? It means that the people of Tanzania have insufficient money. The people pay taxes out of the very little wealth they have; it is from these taxes that the Government meets its recurrent and development expenditure. When we call on the Government to spend more money on development projects, we are asking the Government to use more money and if the Government does not have any more, the only way it can do this is to increase its revenue through extra taxation.

If one calls on the Government to spend more, one is in effect calling on the Government to increase taxes. Calling on the Government to spend more without raising taxes is like demanding that the Government should perform miracles; it is equivalent to asking for more milk from a cow while insisting that the cow should not be milked again. (Julius Nyerere, 'The Arusha Declaration and TANU's Policy on Socialism and Self-Reliance,' 5 February 1967, https://www.marxists.org/subject/africa/nyerere/1967/arusha-declaration.htm.)

30 Translations into English by author.

31 France24 [Youtube channel], 'Francis Kéré, prix Pritzker: 'Je suis honoré et ça m'encourage à continuer mes recherches,' 16 March 2022, https://www.youtube.com/watch?v=6ri1FqcNTHg.

32 France24 [Youtube channel], 'Francis Kéré, prix Pritzker.

33 France24 [Youtube channel], 'Francis Kéré, prix Pritzker.

34 Sankara, 'A United Front Against Debt.'

ABOUT THE AUTHORS

Grieve Chelwa is associate professor of Political Economy and Chair of the Social Sciences Department at the Africa Institute. He is also a senior fellow at Tricontinental: Institute for Social Research. His current research focuses on the political economy of development in Africa. Chelwa has previously held academic and administrative positions at The New School, the University of Cape Town and Harvard University. He holds a PhD in economics from the University of Cape Town.

Marion Ouma is a research associate with the South Africa Research Chair Initiative (SARChI) on Social Policy at the University of South Africa, where she also completed her doctorate. Her research interests include social policy, social protection, policymaking and the political economy of Africa's development. She has been published in Critical Social Policy and Africa Development, with book chapters in The Handbook of African Political Economy and Social Policy in an African Context. She has written several op-eds including for The Daily Nation and Africa Is a Country.

Cleopas Gabriel Sambo is a post-doctoral fellow at Oslo Metropolitan University where his research focuses on the gendered dimensions of social assistance programmes. He is also a lecturer in Social Work & Sociology at the University of Zambia. Samba was a co-editor of The Politics of Welfare in the Global South.

Redge Nkosi is a senior economic advisor to the Coalition for Dialogue on Africa (CoDA). He is the founding director of Monetary Reform International, an organisation aimed at reforming the global monetary and banking system and also the head of research for Firstsource Money – a money, banking and macroeconomic research and advisory group. He holds a master's in economics. Find him on X @redgenkosi.

Ndongo Samba Sylla is a Senegalese development economist. He was a senior research and program manager at the West African office of the Rosa Luxemburg Foundation in Dakar. Sylla is the author of The Fair Trade Scandal: Marketing Poverty to Benefit the Rich and co-authored Africa's Last Colonial Currency: The CFA Franc Story. He is also a co-editor of Economic and Monetary Sovereignty for 21st Century Africa and Revolutionary Movements in Sub-Saharan Africa: An Untold Story as well as the sole editor of Imperialism and the Political Economy of Global South's Debt. Find him on X @nssylla.

ABOUT THE INTERNATIONAL UNION OF LEFT PUBLISHERS

Formed in 2020, the International Union of Left Publishers emerged as a platform for left publishers to promote left books on Red Books Day (21 February), to defend left authors, publishers, and bookshops, and to develop a copyleft method of sharing books across our countries and languages. There are approximately 30 publishers in our union.

Our previous joint books are *Ruth First: Selected Writings*, *Lenin 150*, *Mariátegui*, *Che*, *Paris Commune 150*, *Kollontai 150*.

You can learn more about the IULP here: https://iulp.org/about.

The publishers that make up the union are 1804 Books, Batalla de Ideas, Bharathi Puthakalayam, Editorial Caminos del Centro Martin Luther King, Chintha Publishers, Editorial El Colectivo, Editorial La Trinchera, Expressão Popular, Gono Prokash, Idea, Inkani Books, Instituto Simón Bolívar, International Publishers, Janashakti, Kriya, LeftWord Books, Marjin Kiri, Naked Punch, National Book Agency India, Nava Telangana, Ojas, Prajasakhti, Red Star Press, Tricontinental: Institute for Social Research, Vadell Hnos Editores, Vam Prakashan, Yordam Kitap, Založba /*cf.